GROWING UP SMALL

GROWING UP SMALL

A HANDBOOK FOR SHORT PEOPLE

BY

Kate Gilbert Phifer

PAUL S. ERIKSSON, *Publisher*
MIDDLEBURY, VERMONT

© 1979 by Kate Gilbert Phifer.
All rights reserved. No part of
this book may be reproduced in any
form without permission of the
Publisher, Paul S. Eriksson,
Middlebury, Vermont 05753. Published
simultaneously in Canada by George
J. McLeod, Toronto, Ontario.

Printed in the United States of America

Library of Congress Cataloging in
Publication Data

Phifer, Kate G   1937–
  Growing up small.

  Includes index.
  1. Human growth. 2. Stature—Psychological
aspects. I. Title.
QP84.P53 1978   612.6   78–11290
ISBN 0–8397–3136–1

For my daughters,
CATHERINE SARAH
and
LINDA GAIL,
who are growing up small and beautiful

Special thanks and recognition
for their generous time, cooperation
and assistance, to Sally Hess,
Dr. William Hoffman, and
the Human Growth Foundation

Contents

	Introduction	3
1	Prejudice Against Short People	6
2	How a Body Grows	21
3	Should You Worry About Your Child's Height?	46
4	Human Growth Hormone	80
5	Effects of Eating and Loving	103
6	Genetics and Height	118
7	The Little People	143
8	Non-Growing Pains	160
9	I Like Being Short	183
	Appendix	202
	Index	*205*

GROWING UP SMALL

Introduction

How *short* are you? That's what people really mean when they ask me, "How *tall* are you?" But short, in our society, is an insult. Short is untall.

I'm 4'9" short. I thought I was 4'10", but while doing research for this book I learned the proper way to measure height, so I tried it. I couldn't stretch one fraction above 4'9" without cheating. Am I shrinking already, at age 41? Maybe I always cheated when I was measured during my "terrible teens."

But I do know this: that one-inch difference is HUGE. Saying "I'm four-ten" had become as natural and as acceptable to my own self image as "I'm female" or "I have red hair." Now I should say "four-nine" which sounds different, and wow, does it ever sound short! It makes me aware of my height. So has writing this book. I was more comfortable with my size last year when I assumed I was 4'10" and I was writing about horse racing!

So why write about being short? The idea first bloomed because so many people—even strangers in the supermarket—questioned me. "How tall are you?" frequently leads to "Does it bother you?" "How can I help my short child cope?" Or, "Where do you buy clothes?" And from children comes the candid, curious: "Are you a midget?"

As I began to explore the ramifications of being short, those questions led to many of my own. How does the normal growth process work, and what slows it down or stops it? What are the danger signals of abnormal growth that parents should watch for? What are the latest discoveries in the causes and cures of short stature? Can parents help their short children grow more? What are the psychological problems? How does our society treat short people—and why? What are the solutions to these problems, both physically and emotionally?

One of the many people I contacted was Brian Morris, an achondroplastic dwarf and an officer of Little People of America, Inc. When I explained the nature of the book and said I was deeply interested in the subject because of all the problems I'd had as a child growing up much shorter than average, Brian looked at me with amazement.

"It's hard for me to believe you ever had any problems! To compare you to me is like comparing a man with a limp to a man with both legs amputated."

That's when it hit me that there are really two extremes of growing up small: my way, of being much shorter than average but physically normal and proportioned, and Brian's way, of being even shorter than I and also disproportionate.

Brian labels me "average short" and there are millions more like me in the U.S. According to a 1976 HEW study, the average adult American female height is just a hair less than 5'5". Over one-half of our adult population of 150 million is female, so at least thirty-seven and a half million are under 5'5". Another government survey has reported that 14 million American women stand between 4'8" and 5'3" and weigh between 85 and 115 pounds.

And the men? Well, the average American male is now 5'9.2". Our macho society is so hyped on bigger is better that even 5'8" men consider themselves short. With probably about thirty-five million of our male population below average, that's a lot of shorties out there.

So, as I said before, how short are you? Are you one of the millions of average short? Are you one of the thousands of little people like Brian Morris? Or did you pick up this book because one of your children is in the group of about 500,000 American children with growth problems?

For all of us short people, young and old, this book is a sharing—of ideas, of research, of feelings. Together let's explore the subject of growing up small: how to understand it, how to cope with it, how to take advantage of it.

1 Prejudice Against Short People

> *What a man sees in the human race is merely himself in the deep and honest privacy of his own heart.*
> Mark Twain

Shortness is the butt of jokes from teasing the littlest kids on the playground or laughing at the circus midgets to singing Randy Newman's "Short People." The song lambasts the shortcomings of short people, equating little minds with little noses and little teeth and repeatedly proclaiming "short people got no reason to live." Newman defends the piece as a satire on prejudice and points out the line "short people are just the same as you and I," but somehow that part gets buried under the insults of "nasty little feet," etc.

After the record's release during the fall of 1977, short people all over the country gasped in disbelief at what their ears were hearing. They didn't think it was funny, and the flood of complaints from the furious short public forced many radio stations to ban the record. Of course the attention it received only made people more interested, and where it wasn't banned it was played so frequently it zoomed to the top of the popular song charts.

Many enterprising short people composed clever "tall people" rebuttals, which helped to bring some humor into the controversial issue. Two "less-tall" entertainers, singer Steve Lawrence and comedian Tim Conway, dreamed up a riotous version about "giant ears and billboard faces, elephant teeth with great big spaces . . ."

Of course the print media added fuel to the fire. The *Wall Street Journal* headlined its article: "Certain Song Makes Short People Stand Tall in Rage." *People* magazine's bold type questioned, "Is Randy Newman's First Gold Hit Just a Short Rib (As He Says) Or His Unkindest Cut of All?" *People* quotes Gerald Rasa, president of Little People of America, as saying, "We're geared to a bigger-is-better society, and this song reinforces that concept."

Virtually every newspaper and magazine had its say, and the topic was such hot news that Rasa, a dedicated p.r. man for little people, was contacted by more than fifty reporters. "What do you think about the Short People record?" became an overused question, to put it politely.

However, I agree with John Hickey, then president of the Human Growth Foundation, who commented to me that at least everyone was thinking about short people, and that's a giant step forward for HGF's goal of public awareness. Through talk shows on radio and TV and "Letters to the Editor" in newspapers and magazines, all the short people could speak up. They said: of course the song's silly, but this is what I really think about being short—here's what it's like for me. And it's wonderful for all of us to have the opportunity to call the world's attention to us, even though we can't see over the lectern.

The whole episode points out a few major insights about short people:

One—there is prejudice against us.
Two—we are often very vulnerable and quickly lose our sense of humor when our size is criticized.
Three—there's a great need for public awareness of, shall we call it, the plight of the untall!

All the flack has been great for the cause. I love the editorial that stated: "If short people follow the well-blazed trail of minority activism in the United States, we may see such signs of progress as . . . a spate of message movies with such titles as 'Short in the Saddle' and 'Little Small Man'."

Americans seem to be so hung up on height that one sociologist has coined a new "ism" to go along with all the others, such as racism, militarism and sexism. Saul Feldman of Case Western Reserve University in Cleveland calls it "heightism."

At a meeting of the American Sociological Association Feldman said, "The rhetoric of the joys of being tall and the evils of being short are well demonstrated in our daily language. The ideal man is viewed as tall, dark and handsome. Impractical people are short-sighted, dishonest cashiers short-change customers, electrical failures are known as short-circuits . . ."

I'm sure you can think of other examples from our daily language—like "small talk." My friends are having a great time asking me if this is a short book! If so, does that make it insignificant?

In this country big is better, whether it refers to cars, houses or people. And as the average American height gets taller, the shorties seem even shorter.

What is the average height? According to an HEW study released the spring of '76, the average American male height at age 18 is 5'9.2", and the female is just under 5'5". According to the Human Growth Foundation, fifty years ago the average adult male was 5'7" tall—more than 2 inches shorter than today. It's easy to see in any museum that the suit of armor from the middle ages is too small for the average modern man. The experts say that the increase in height is due primarily to improved nutrition, the reduction of many childhood illnesses and a cross-breeding of different population groups.

People are not only growing taller, but they're growing at a faster rate than ever before. Fifty years ago it wasn't unusual to keep growing until age 26 or more. Today the maximum height is usually reached by males at 18 and females at 16. Faster growth rate means that our kids have fewer years to imitate Jack's beanstalk. The body must perform its glorious trick of growing taller at an early age, or shorty will be branded forever.

This matter of height and the prejudice against the lack of it is, of course, relative. What height is short? Perhaps to you, five feet two is short, but to me five feet two is not short at all. We all have a height, like it or not. Doctors measure it in centimeters while the rest of us are still thinking inches. In a world where a distance of 2500 miles from New York to San Francisco has been reduced to a three-and-a-half hour plane flight, a distance of a mere inch of height can be an unbridgeable gap and source of envy and despair. For many years my goal in life was to grow to a height of 5 feet. I missed it by the length of a standard lipstick tube—three inches. Insignificant? Infinitessimal? Wrong! Haven't you seen two children stand back to back and argue at length over which one was taller, even though a few hairs were the only difference? Of course neither one wants to be the shorter! Nevertheless, it is these small differences between human beings that make each of us distinct and unique.

Height is an extremely vital ingredient to our concept of ourselves and of the world around us. Although each of us knows approximately what our height measurement is (no cheating!), we're usually not aware of it as such, because we have no control over it, like we do our hair styles or the way we dress. As adults we are so used to how our bodies feel in relation to other people and things that we don't think about it. But stand on a chair or squat and you can see how different heights give different perspectives—and a whole new identity of you.

As Dr. Seymour Fisher explains in his book, *Body Consciousness: You Are What You Feel,* "because your body is psychologically closer to you (being indistinguishable from your identity or existence) than any other object, it serves as a unique screen upon which you project your concerns and wishes." In other words, the body is a tool which we use to interpret and understand our environment. Your height will affect your feelings about your surroundings and other people. Anyone, no matter how tall, will feel small in a large space like the open sea or a great concert hall. And even I felt tall when I cradled my first infant.

Dr. Fisher also points out that the way people react to your height affects your sense of identity, your feeling of self. Which brings us back to our society's view of short stature which links little legs with little minds. Even according to Webster, if you are short you are "not long enough"—you lack height, you are deficient. This reaction inevitably influences your self-image. If you not only look small but also feel small, you'll have a tough row to hoe. Like my husband tells me, "You don't have to act small just because you were born that way."

Our association with growing up and growing taller is very tight, and is the source of much of the prejudice.

Watching little Johnnie and Suzy grow big and tall is a tradition as American as apple pie. Proud parents lovingly measure each succeeding inch, beginning at birth. Baby's weight and length are imprinted for posterity on birth certificate and announcements, and Mama lovingly records them in the baby book. When mothers stroll their buggies to the park and ooh and aah over each other's offspring, they compare increases in weight because at that stage of development weight is the common indicator of growth.

When the child walks, height becomes more important. I'm sure growth charts are common in many families. The kids line up, feet without shoes, heels pressed back against the wall or door, back straight. The ruler goes flat on the head, and the pencil mark is drawn with date and initials alongside. Then the comparison starts. "Oh look! I've grown an inch," or "Gee, I thought you'd grown more than that," or "Wow, I've grown three inches since last fall!"

Growth indicates health, so parents are convinced that bigger growth means better health. It's one of parents' few concrete, positive signs that they are doing a good job, and they need that reassurance. If their child isn't growing tall, is it their fault? They're afraid so. If a child can't reach far enough up the wall to fulfill his parents' expectations, he wonders, "What is wrong with me?" Like Charlie Brown, both child and parents have failure feelings.

One of the biggest stigmas to being small is that we equate growing with maturing, not only physically but mentally. Dr.

John Money, a psychologist who specializes in dwarfism, says, "All human beings have an automatic, unthinking capacity to orient themselves toward other people on the basis of stature and physique as indexes of age and mental maturity." He notes that even parents and physicians have this problem when they're alerted to it. Children who are taller than average are expected to be more mature than their friends, and suffer for it just as much as short children who are assumed to be at lower intelligence and emotional levels, as well as physical, compared to their taller friends.

The shortest kid in the class doesn't need a psychologist or a scientific study to tell him or her that there is prejudice in our society against being short. Kids learn very early how their size relates to their potential. For example, when elementary school children choose up sides for a team, whether for baseball, relay races, or playing jump rope, nobody wants the littlest kid. I used to stand there in utter agony waiting to be chosen. Children are openly honest, and when they don't want you, they sure let you know it.

Small kids are reminded every day at school about just how short they are. One of the favorite pastimes is "I can pick you up." Usually the kids don't even ask—they just grab and lift. I was always at least a head shorter than my peers, and I was often suddenly dangling helplessly in mid air—a sign to my attacker of her own strength and superiority over me. Everyone thought it was so cute and funny. There are many cases of severely stunted children being carried around from class to class and treated like dolls.

Elementary school children are also reminded of their shortness by their teachers. Like lining up. Always it's the shortest first, whether they're going for a march down the hall to the bathroom, going on a field trip, or lining up for a picture or a dance. Inevitably the teacher says, "shortest over here!"

There are many physical features of the school world that are too high for short kids. There's the challenge of reaching the blackboard. How would you feel if you could reach only a foot above the chalk ledge? But one man's poison is always another's meat. My five-foot daughter Cathy stood on a chair in high school chemistry class to work long problems on the board and she loved the special attention.

On the playground the monkeybars are too high, and in the coat room the hooks are too high. Dangling feet are a perpetual pain at any age. I'll never forget the time when I was in the fifth or sixth grade, I was sitting in a classroom and the janitor interrupted the class, which was most unusual. He was carrying a little stool that he had made. He came over to me, put the stool down on the floor under my feet and said, "Now you will be more comfortable." He thought that he was doing me a favor, and in a sense he certainly was. However, once again my size was pointed out to everybody, and they all had a big laugh. It always helps to have a good sense of humor—especially when you're short!

These physical drawbacks exist not only in school but also at home. How about closet rods, bathroom mirrors, and speaking of bathrooms, how about toilets? Do you know what it's like to have a bowel movement when your feet don't reach the floor? I'll bet your short child does. Try it—you won't like it.

In many homes while the children are young and are expected to be shorter than adults, many features of the home are adjusted to make it easier for kids. But then a point is reached sometime when the child is in junior or senior high when he is expected to have "grown up" and these aids are taken away whether the child is ready physically to do without them or not. For example, sitting at a regular dining table may be very uncomfortable, but when the child gets too old to use a junior chair, the parents often assume he no longer needs it and take it away, and the child silently suffers. I solved that problem when I was old enough to buy my own dining table; I had a carpenter cut the legs down a couple of inches. Now, it's more comfortable for me, and I don't think anyone notices that it's shorter than the average dining table.

Outside the home the world is definitely constructed by tall engineers. High pay phones. Top shelves in super markets.

Reaching the gas pedal and seeing over the steering wheel at the same time. Reaching your mouth up to a drinking fountain. Yes, each physical problem sounds insignificant, but molehills combine to make mountains.

The psychological pitfalls are far worse than the physical ones. Trite remarks like "How's the weather down there?", "Get out of that hole", "You can stand up now", and "Hey, shrimp", are commonplace reminders of the vast pressure against you. One of the more original labels in my case, due to my red hair, was "Fireplug."

The time of most agony for short people is junior and senior high schools. There is wide variance in the age of the adolescent growth spurt, and a lot of kids who eventually reach average height are very short in their early teenage years. The unfortunate part is that many parents don't even realize what their children are experiencing. They may notice that their child is a little short for his or her age, but from their adult point of view, they know time flies and they believe with utmost confidence that by the time he finishes school he will grow. So the parents say, "Don't worry, you'll shoot up overnight."

What the parents don't realize is that the kid doesn't care what's going to happen five years from now, or two years from now or even a year from now . . . what they care about is *now*. They are short *now*, and it's hard to conceive that in five years they won't be short. Five years to them is like forever. So their problems are now, when the prejudice is probably the strongest. Adolescents have one goal, and that is to be like everybody else. If their height sets them apart, then they are automatically segregated in every way, in athletics, in social life, and in the academic life too.

In junior and senior high school, the boys are probably affected more by their shortness than the girls because of status in sports. Every father wants his son to be a football or basketball or baseball player, and mother goes along with this attitude. The best athletes get the best girls as well as special consideration from the teachers. If a boy is excluded from

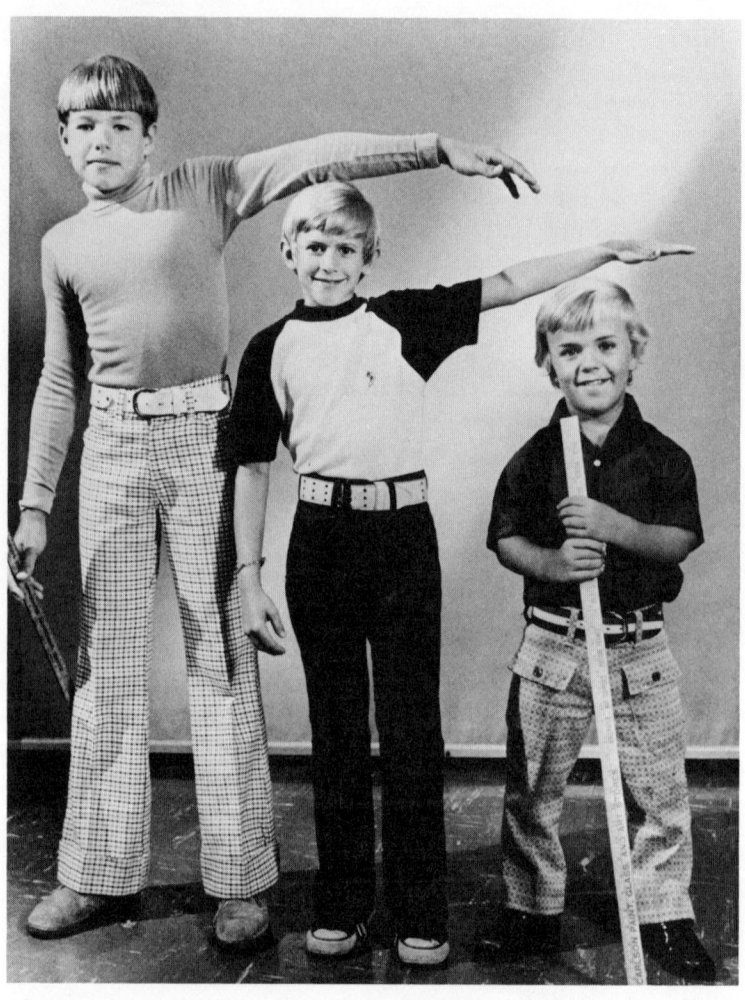

Three 12-year-old boys—average, hypopituitary, and achondroplastic
(Photo courtesy of Human Growth Foundation)

these sports because of his size, the psychological handicap may not be erased with a later growth spurt.

A friend of mine who is now a successful dermatologist and a handsome 5'9", was 4'11" when he started high school. Eager to begin his football career, his hopes and most of his self-confidence were trampled when the coach looked at him briefly and quipped, "Come back when you grow up." The summer after his sophomore year he grew eight inches, but his new, acceptable height didn't erase the two years of rejection. He told me that all he thought about during that time was his fierce desire to grow and it affected his whole life, including his studies. Now he admits that the experience helped him to become an understanding doctor.

Slow growth is sometimes associated with slow sexual maturation, which can lead to its own problems at the teenage stage. However, shortness does not necessarily mean sexual immaturity or inability. My menstruation cycles began at age 12, when I was about four and a half feet tall. When I was a senior I was going hot and heavy with a boy who abruptly stopped dating me. His father ended the relationship because he thought I was too short to bear children. (P.S. My two daughters arrived in natural births; Cathy weighed six pounds and Linda 5 pounds 12 ounces.)

For girls, being short frequently means being cute, but never pretty. A short girl cannot be willowy, slender, gorgeous or sophisticated. Long is lovely and big is beautiful. A short girl can be petite, peppy, cuddly, also pudgy, plump and chunky. All our ads on TV say so.

The kids themselves support heightism, because they have a very acute sense of what's "normal" and are very skeptical about anyone who differs from the norm. I've had a couple of different experiences that point this factor out.

When Linda was in the fifth grade, she became acutely aware that I was much shorter than her friends' mothers. Suddenly her friends noticed that they were as tall or taller than Linda's mother, and this produced a lot of comment that Linda didn't like. She would passionately defend me and yet hated to be put in the position to have to do so. So at that time, in all innocence and without meaning to hurt me, she asked me not to come to her school because she didn't want her friends to see me. This was her way of dealing with the prejudice. I must add that by the time she was in the eighth grade my short height no longer bothered her, and at 5'2" she loves towering over me.

The other experience occurred when I was 19 and a counselor at a summer camp in Vermont. In my cabin I had five 12-year-olds. Now, at 4'9" I am about average height for a fifth grader, about age 10 to 11. All five of these 12-year-olds were much taller than I. When they first saw me, they were very wary of me—there was a tremendous tension between us. I had to work extra hard to get them to trust me and to respect me. Kids don't respect people who are littler than they are. Adults react the same way. When we look up to someone, we respect them, automatically. The person may later prove unworthy of respect, but until then just the physical action of looking up to someone's face produces a feeling of esteem. Conversely, to look down on someone makes us question their ability in every sense—their mental ability as well as their physical ability. You have to prove yourself if people look down on you. In fact, the words "look down" mean to disapprove. And this is certainly what happened to me that summer as a camp counselor.

Not only will a taller person command more respect, but an esteemed person will actually appear taller. This scientific phenomenon is known as psychological or perceived height. To prove it, an Australian scientist introduced one man to five different groups of students. The first group of students was told that he was a fellow student, the second a sort of teacher's aid, the third a lecturer, the fourth a senior lecturer, and the fifth a college professor. After each introduction the man left the room and the group was asked to estimate his height. Each group overestimated, but the first group pegged the "student" 2½ inches shorter than the last group estimated the "professor." The groups in between fell along the predicted curve and judged his height according to the amount of status and authority he supposedly had.

This automatic pull in favor of tall people is reflected in the job market. The University of Pittsburgh, for example, recently surveyed some of its graduates and discovered that men over 6 feet 2 started at salaries 12.4% higher than the amount paid to graduates under 6 feet.

In another study, an Eastern Michigan University professor asked 140 business recruiters to choose between two equally qualified job applicants, one of whom stood 5'5", and the other 6'1". More than 70% hired (hypothetically) the taller man. Only 1% said they would take on the shorter man. The others professed not to care. Other studies show that tall men rise through the executive hierarchy of the corporate structure faster, start from higher positions, and earn more money.

The accepted image of a successful businessman being tall is what bothers my five-foot-seven brother and many other men about being short. To go the same distance a short man must run twice as far. That's why many of the few top executives who are short are often accused of Napoleon power-complexes, such as a little guy in my neighborhood who said, "I'll show the world how big I am" and proceeded to build an empire that handles unedible merchandise in supermarkets, like potato peelers.

The concept of successful TALL businessmen was obvious to me the other day when I was fortunate to have a tour of the new executive office building at the world headquarters of Bendix Corporation. The Board Room is exquisite in every detail. Covering the center of the floor is a gorgeous aqua carpet, intricately woven with multi-color flowers and leaves. There is no long table, as in movie board rooms. Instead, a large clear-glass table sits at one end of the carpet in front of an aqua, tufted-velvet swivel arm-chair. There are about 15 more aqua, tufted-velvet, swivel arm-chairs positioned in a rectangle around that gorgeous carpet. And you know what? Those chairs are HUGE! They're tall, wide, deep and high.

(Obviously made for tall men with wide experience, deep convictions and high intelligence—right?) Heaven forbid any 5'3" man (or woman!) should aspire to sit in that imposing room with any dignity. I don't mean to pick on Bendix; I'm sure all board rooms are alike in that respect and I know chairs in lawyers' offices usually are extra imposing also, not to mention other professions.

Politics reflects our bias too. Since 1900 only two major-party presidential candidates who were shorter than their opponents have been elected: Calvin Coolidge and Jimmy Carter.

We've had one very small President. James Madison was 5'4" and weighed under 100 pounds. That wasn't considered as small in 1809 as it is today, but Washington Irving described him as "a withered little apple-john." It's interesting to note that our smallest President, popularly nicknamed "Jemmy," was the only President to face enemy gunfire while in office. When the British invaded Washington in the War of 1812, Jemmy personally took command of an artillery battery.

Of course the shorter you are the harder it is to measure up. If you think life can be tough for the 5'2" male, how about the 4'3" achondroplastic dwarf? The problems are magnified a thousand-fold. Finding a job, finding a mate, and just finding a new pair of shoes are major dilemmas.

Medically speaking, dwarfs and midgets are bracketed together within the syndrome called dwarfism. Joan Weiss is a clinical social worker at Johns Hopkins University's Moore Clinic, which specializes in genetic growth problems. In her recent paper on "The Social Development of Dwarfs" she states the generally held medical opinion, "Dwarfism is equated with a failure to achieve a height of 4'10" at maturity," and estimates that there are approximately 100,000 dwarfs in this country.

So that means I'm a dwarf. How do I feel about that label? Well, like most other dwarfs, I'd rather be called little, short, or small. Actually, I guess the correct label for me is midget, and all the kids in the supermarket who stare at me would quickly agree. Midgets have proportionate short stature and dwarfs are disproportionately short statured. But I'm pretty tall for a midget, according to the 2500 members of the Little People of America, Inc. Most of the members of LPA are dwarfs, but they call themselves little people and their dwarf children are "little littles."

Labels are very important to little people, and the attitudes reveal a prejudice within a prejudice. Dr. Charles Scott, who is chairman of LPA's Medical Advisory Board and director of the genetics clinic at the University of Texas, reports that, "In working with little people it can be a costly social blunder to mistakenly use the word 'midget' in reference to a person who is actually dwarfed . . . Even short children of only 5 years use these terms carefully. One disproportionate little girl became incensed with a playmate who had called her a midget and an elf . . . 'I am a dwarf, not a midget—so there!' "

In preparing this book I've learned that there's a gulf between the dwarfs or little people and the average short. It seems to me that many dwarfs are somewhat put off by the average short. They don't mind tall people or even average-sized people because their worlds are so dissimilar that they can hardly identify with each other. But to be an average short . . . ah, that's a life a dwarf can imagine and yearn for but never achieve.

Conversely, I think frequently an average short person feels more intolerance for a dwarf than does a tall person. A five-foot male doesn't want—EVER—to be confused with a dwarf or midget. Even short people who are severely affected by the heightist feelings in our society will turn around and shower those same prejudices against those less tall than they.

So I will try to use my terms carefully and not offend anyone. If you and/or your children are average short and you are wondering if this book is just about dwarfs—it's not. If you and/or your children are "little people" and you're wondering if this book is just about the average short—it's not. Let's try to put prejudice aside, and learn from and about each other.

The dominating feature of being short is that we must live

in a world that is physically and psychologically geared for taller people. We are different, and anyone who is different from the American ideal image suffers—be it the short, tall, fat, skinny, black, hunch-backed, etc.

This world isn't going to change for us. Yes, it certainly helps for the public to be more aware and tolerant of our difficulties and in these days of equal-opportunity laws and regulations for helping and hiring the handicapped it's easier to be short than it was fifty years ago. All minorities have it easier now—women, blacks, and even dwarfs. But everyone always likes to look down on someone, and there will always be a pecking order. Dad picks on Mom, who picks on Child, who picks on Dog, who picks on Cat, who picks on Rat. And short people will always be at the bottom of the heap.

How can we overcome this problem and achieve social adjustment and self-acceptance? By growing. Taller, if possible, but more important by growing mentally and emotionally. Stature has more than one dimension.

2 How a Body Grows

> *A man's legs should be long enough to reach the ground.*
> Abraham Lincoln

As Alice in Wonderland said, growth is "curiouser and curiouser," but we don't shoot up to nine feet tall by gobbling down a piece of cake marked "Eat Me." The normal growth process of the human body involves a complexity of interwoven factors, and scientists are understanding more of its mysteries every day. The study of growth and development contains the whole arena of increase in size, differentiation of structure and change of form. The human adult bears more resemblance to a fetus than the oak tree to an acorn, but in the same way the change is profound.

All systems of our bodies are interrelated, and the growth and development of one part will affect all the other parts. For example, neurologic growth (the nervous system and the brain) has its own growth pattern, and so do the genitalia and the lymph glands. But the overall mechanisms of growth require specific events and specific timing, so that the whole show goes off without a hitch. If one event is missing or mistimed during the formation of organs in the body during certain stages, an organ may be malformed or lose all potential for normal growth and development. Recent studies of embryogenesis (growth of the embryo) have shown that cell development depends in part on the development of surrounding cells. Therefore, a thorough understanding of the body's growth process requires a study of every part of the body. But what we're interested in is: why are people short?

So, from the whole slew of human growth and development factors, I'm going to select the ingredients that particularly influence our height, and in this chapter let's see how the average, run-of-the-mill human body grows *up*.

We all start as a single fertilized cell, the combination of an ovum and a sperm, and by adulthood the average body contains about 100 trillion cells. After the incredibly rapid growth period before birth, most full-term babies come into the world at essentially the same birth length of 20 inches, give or take an inch. In the first years of life there is very rapid height increase, then a slowing down, then a spurt of growth at puberty and finally a trailing off at maturity.

Dr. Robert M. Blizzard, a pioneer in investigating and treating problems of growth failure and presently chief of pediatrics at the University of Virginia Hospital, has outlined the basic American growth pattern this way: "The average infant measures 20 inches at birth and grows half as much in the first year of life as he did in utero—namely 10 inches. In the second year he adds half of that—5 inches—and half of that—2½ inches—every year thereafter until puberty at about 12 years."

Thus, at 4 years a child is about 40 inches or twice his birth length; at 8 years about 50 inches; and at 12 years approximately 60 inches. Growth rates are similar for boys and girls until puberty, and as the child advances into adolescence the adolescent growth spurt occurs, which is related to the presence of growth hormone and the increased production of the sex hormones. Puberty is the only time that there is an acceleration of linear growth. This height spurt differs between the sexes in duration, amount and velocity. We'll look at this rate of growth from baby to adult in more detail in the next chapter, but first, let's examine a little of the body chemistry that sparks the growth machine. The three key factors that we'll cover in this chapter are genes, hormones and bones.

Genes

Genes are the chemical units we inherit from our parents that direct our biological growth from conception to death. Every living organism has its unique set of genes. I have mine, you have yours, the strawberry begonia hanging at my window has its, the majestic elm tree across the street has another unique set of genes, and so does my tabby cat, Smuckers Butterscotch, who loves to spread his gorgeous body all over my desk so I can't write. Only identical twins have identical genes. In chapter six we'll take a close look at how this genetic material is passed from parents to child, but in this chapter let's find out what genes are and how this essential chemical information, called the genetic code, directs the body's growth.

Most of us learned in biology class that genes are components of chromosomes, which exist in pairs. Every different kind of plant or animal has its characteristic number of chromosomes in the nucleus of each cell (except the ova and sperm cells); fruit flies have 8 and we humans have 46, arranged in 23 pairs.

It wasn't until the middle of this century that biochemists began to discover the chemical composition of chromosomes. The story of the discovery reads like the best mystery-suspense novel, and I highly recommend *The Double Helix* by James D. Watson. In 1953, two imaginative young scientists, James Watson and Francis Crick, built their celebrated laboratory model revealing the molecular structure of deoxyribonucleic acid (DNA) which culminated 50 years of work by many scientists. Their excitement was contagious, and Watson wrote about how Crick told "everyone within hearing distance that we had found the secret of life." And they had, for chromosomes consist of DNA. In the years since then, their work has been proved not only correct but also one of the epic discoveries in the history of scientific thought.

DNA is the fundamental chemical unit of life, and therefore, of growth. Genes are pieces of this DNA material, and in order to understand how they work it's necessary to have a conception of the basic structure of DNA. It is made up of only five common elements: hydrogen, oxygen, carbon, nitrogen and phosphorus. These elements are combined into six different groups which are arranged in what Watson described as "a beautiful new structure" because of its simplicity.

Look at my sketch (Fig. 1) and think of a ladder. The sides are composed of two alternating groups called sugar (deoxyribose) and phosphate groups. The rungs are composed of four different groups called nitrogen bases: adenine, thymine, guanine and cytosine (abbreviated A,C,T and G). Each rung contains two bases, and adenine always pairs with thymine, while guanine always pairs with cytosine. That is, an A will make a rung only with a T, and a C only with a G. So that A-T, T-A, C-G and G-C pairs are like four letters of an alphabet, and they are arranged in an almost endless variation of sequence within each giant DNA molecule. The rungs attach to the sides at the sugar groups, so the phosphate groups are opposite the open spaces between the rungs.

Now, pretend the ladder is firmly based so that an imaginary center axis remains straight, and pretend to take the tops of the two sides and twist them. Now what kind of a shape do you have? A double helix (see sketch). It is the particular sequence of the A-T, T-A, C-G, G-C alphabet on each winding strand of DNA that determines the unique characteristics of each living organism. It is this sequence of bases that is the language of the genetic code, and we each have our own unique code. A geneticist once estimated that the number of different ways of putting together all the A's, T's, C's and G's in a set of human chromosomes would be the figure of 256 followed by 2.4 billion zeros. So, you see, each of us is an unbelievable long shot!

A single molecule of DNA may contain several thousand crosslinks, and within the core of living cells enormously long strands of DNA intertwine. In a fascinating article, "The Awesome Worlds Within a Cell" (Sept. 1976), *National Geographic Magazine* points out that if all the DNA in the cells of a human body were untwisted and joined end-to-end, they would reach

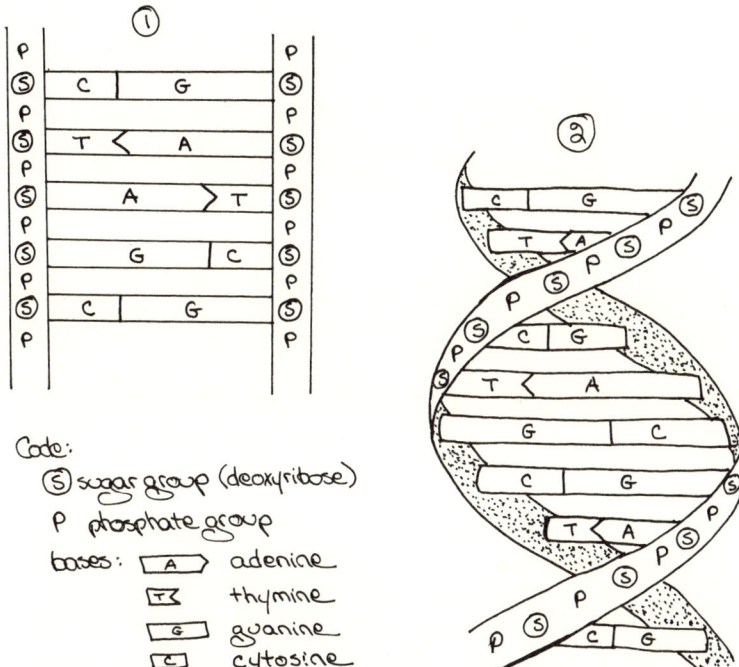

Fig. 1. Simplified sketches showing a piece of the double-helix structure of DNA (2) and the "ladder" construction if the figure is straightened out (1). Notice how the bases are paired, T and A always together and likewise C and G. The order and arrangement of these bases differ in every individual (except identical twins), so that each of us has his or her own "genetic code." When conception occurs the structure of the cell's DNA is established in the 46 chromosomes, and as the body grows and develops throughout life the genetic code in every body cell is identical.

from the earth to the sun and back 400 times. But in its natural state, this same quantity of DNA is so tightly coiled that it would fit in a box the size of an ice cube.

A gene is a section of a chromosome that controls a specific piece of information, such as eye color. A gene may consist of perhaps 500 to 2,000 rungs of the DNA ladder—no one knows yet how many, nor how many genes a human cell contains.

Estimates range from as low as a total of 10,000 genes for all the chromosomes to as high as 20,000 for each individual chromosome.

At the time of conception a person's full complement of DNA, his entire genetic code, is packed within the fertilized egg. From that moment on until death every time a cell divides to form two new cells, the DNA duplicates itself. Therefore every cell of the body contains an exact copy of the complete genetic code.

Do you remember learning about cell division, the process of mitosis, in biology? When a cell divides, the DNA molecule splits up the middle and doubles itself in a process called replication. Instead of a ladder, now think of the double helix as a zipper. Each tooth is a base unit. The chemical bond of the teeth joined to the sides is very strong, but the hydrogen bond between the teeth is weak and easily opens, unzipping the zipper (see Fig. 2). As these weak hydrogen bonds between the base pairs melt, the coil unwinds, making two long chains. The single bases remain attached to the backbone of the sugar and phosphate groups. Circulating in the dividing cell are freely moving, unattached base units which are attracted to the chains. They find their proper places, A always joining with T and G with C, and the molecule is completed with a new sugar-phosphate chain. Thus each half builds a new opposite, making two new DNA molecules exactly like the original one. By this process of replication, the same genetic code is passed on to each cell of your body as it grows and renews itself throughout life. The same process also passes on part of your genetic code to your children, as we'll see later in chapter six, when we concentrate more on genetics.

DNA is the "secret of life" because it directs the protein-building function of the cells, and protein (from a Greek word meaning "holding first place") is the key to growth. Each gene contains instructions for making one specific protein, and there are an estimated 50,000 to 100,000 different proteins in your body. Proteins are giant molecules made up of many amino acid building blocks, typically sev-

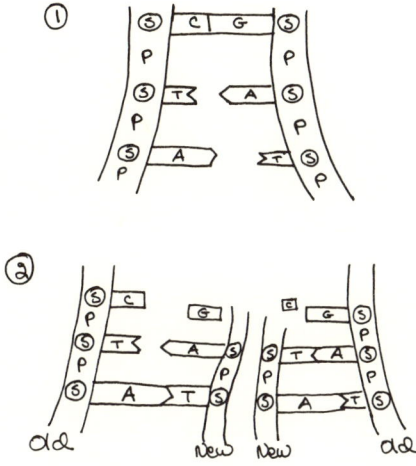

Fig. 2. A simplified version of replication of DNA: (1) The DNA "zipper" unzips. (2) Free-moving bases attach to the bases remaining on each side of the original chain, keeping the same sequence, and a new sugar-phosphate chain is formed, resulting in two DNA chains identical to the original one.

eral hundred and even several thousand. But the human body utilizes only twenty-three different amino acids in its protein synthesis, so no wonder we need trillions of cells to do all that protein building.

Apart from water, proteins are the most important group of compounds in the body, accounting for three-fourths of its dry weight. Every tissue, muscle, organ, structure of the body including skin, nails and hair is built with protein, and production of new protein molecules is growth at its most fundamental level.

How does the DNA in the cell nucleus direct the cell to build proteins? The chemical process works similarly to the way DNA duplicates itself in cell division—the bases unzip, but this time just a small portion. Say for example that a cell is signalled to

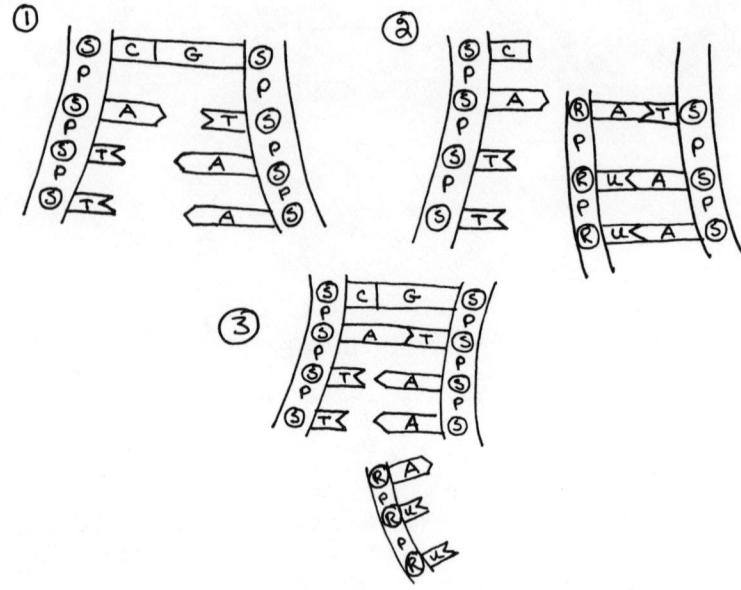

Fig. 3. Transcription of RNA from DNA (a simplified version): (1) A segment of DNA splits apart. (2) Free-floating bases pair with one side of the DNA chain, with Uracil (U) replacing Thymine (T), and in the new backbone the sugar group is ribose instead of deoxyribose. (3) The single-stranded RNA detaches, and the original DNA segment zips back up. The RNA carries its "coded message" to the cell's protein factory.

make more toenail, so only the part of the DNA that codes for toenail protein unzips. Free-floating nitrogen bases copy the sequence of the bases by attaching themselves in proper order, C with G, A with—whoops—not T this time but U (uracil). In this process called transcription (see Fig. 3) instead of forming another strand of DNA, another nucleic acid is formed—ribonucleic acid (RNA) in which the base thymine is replaced by uracil and the sugar group is ribose instead of deoxyribose. This new strand of RNA unzips and the piece of DNA recloses.

The single-strand RNA (called messenger RNA) is carried away to a ribosome in the cytoplasm of the cell to be copied again. In this step another type of RNA called transfer RNA receives the chemical message and brings the right amino acids—the building blocks of protein—to be hooked together. The order of amino acids in a protein determines the job it performs. Thus the RNA acts like a tape recording of the DNA message, and the instructions are passed on to the cell's protein-building factory, the basis of all growth.

The study of cell chemistry, structure and function of DNA, and protein metabolism is a very complicated puzzle, and I've just pulled apart a few pieces for you to see. The control mechanisms are very complex and scientists are only beginning to understand them. Evidently, once a cell is designated for a certain purpose, such as eye or skin, only the specific genes required to perform the function of that cell can be activated. So, although every cell has a full complement of genes, only specific parts of the code can be transferred. Each living cell follows its own intricate path, knowing when to grow, when to divide, when to build proteins, when to die.

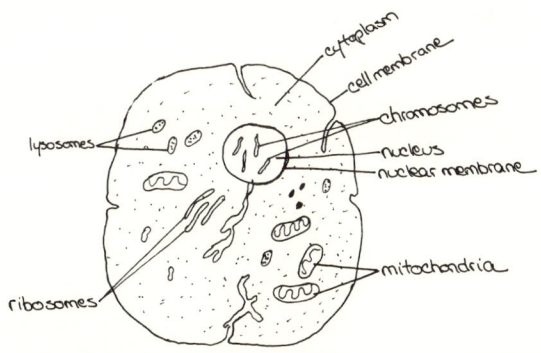

Fig. 4. A few of the many working parts of a human cell that carry on hundreds of different processes. Within the cytoplasm, the jelly-like bulk of the cell, manufacture of protein is carried on by the ribosomes. Energy is supplied by the mitochondria, which move throughout the cytoplasm. Lysosomes are storehouses for enzymes. All functions of the cell are controlled by the nucleus, which is packed with chromosomes.

Not only are your various parts composed of protein molecules, but also their function depends on proteins. A very important example of this category of proteins is enzymes. Did you know that every single one of your body's chemical processes is aided by an enzyme—a *different* enzyme? Just as amazing as how the enzyme rennin changes milk to cheese or how other enzymes make the morning glory open in the morning and close in the afternoon, your enzymes help your body digest food, create energy, build up bone, remove wastes, breathe, even think. You could not live without them, and you certainly couldn't grow.

Enzymes work as catalysts to speed up chemical reactions. According to Melvin Berger in his interesting book *Enzymes In Action*, enzymes don't start chemical reactions, but can only speed them up. However, without enzymes the chemical processes would work too slowly to support life.

Each enzyme is specific for one reaction, and sometimes it needs a helper or coenzyme, which can be a vitamin or hormone. Enzymes are tiny, fragile—and powerful. Berger describes how in the small intestine enzymes break down the protein molecules in food into amino acids. For a chemist to perform the same process he must add a strong acid to the protein and boil it for twenty-four hours. The body enzymes do the same thing in three hours, without strong acids and at normal body temperature.

Scientists are learning more about these fascinating chemicals every day. The first synthetic enzyme was created in a laboratory in 1969. Scientists have also found ways to remove enzymes from the living being that made them and put them to work—washing clothes, preparing food, treating diseases. Drug and soap factories, bakeries, breweries, all sorts of industrial manufacturers now use tons of enzymes that are commercially mass-produced from plant, animal and microbe cells. Berger reports that about $100 million worth of enzymes are sold in the United States every year.

Aside from the commercial uses, enzymes—or the lack of certain ones—have been pinpointed as the cause of malfunctions of the body. For example, PKU (phenylketonuria) is an inherited disease that prevents brain cells from developing normally and results in severe mental retardation. Scientists have discovered that the disease is caused by the lack of the enzyme normally found in the liver that converts phenylalanine in the blood to tyrosine, another animo acid. Without the enzyme, phenylalanine builds up and changes to other chemicals that accumulate in the blood, spinal fluid and urine and eventually affect the brain cells. Scientists found that if the disease was detected soon enough after birth and the infant's diet restricted in phenylanine content, allowing just enough of this essential amino acid to support growth, PKU can be avoided. Now, most states require newborns to be tested for PKU.

It is hoped that continued enzyme research will reveal causes of growth retardation that eventually can be as easily detected and treated as PKU. One thing is certain, enzymes influence the process of growing up—tall or short—just as surely as they help fireflies glow in the dark.

We'll get back to genes and proteins and their influence on growth in later chapters, but now let's look at another category of proteins built from our genetic codes that's intimately associated with growth.

HORMONES

Once I read about comparing growth to the construction of a building. The energetic author related the architect's blueprint to the body's heredity, the framework to the environment, the foreman to the bone structure, and the workmen to the hormones. He hit the nail on the head in the last category, because if the workmen go on strike, the building will not only stop growing, it will probably collapse.

Hormones are proteins produced by the endocrine glands and transported by the blood to their work sites, called target organs. *External* secretions like saliva, milk, tears and urine pour into ducts and are transported outside the body. In contrast, hormones are called *internal* secretions, and endocrine glands are sometimes referred to as the ductless glands. The endocrine system is not neatly joined together like the skeletal or nervous systems, and the various sites of hormone production may be far removed from where the hormone does its work, but all the glands secrete directly into the bloodstream. In fact, transporting hormones is one of the most important functions of the circulatory system. It doesn't do a bad job; blood travels around the body twice in a minute. That's not as fast as the nervous system works though. Nerve impulses flash along at one hundred or more yards per second.

The original Greek word *hormon* means to stir up or excite. And that's just what hormones do to the body. Interacting with the genes and the environment, hormones play a vital role in controlling all aspects of body function. The system as a whole maintains chemical stability within the body. Sometimes hormones work in conjunction with enzymes, vitamins or other chemicals, sometimes they work with each other, and sometimes they perform an independent role. The amount of hormones the glands produce varies from time to time, and often the output from one gland influences output from others.

From birth to maturity, hormones control the rate of growth. Each one of the many different kinds has a specific function, and new research techniques are allowing investigators to study the action of these chemical agents with greater precision than ever before. The biochemical analysis of hormones was revolutionized in the 1960's by the development of radioimmunoassay—a laboratory test that can measure in body fluids one thousandth the amount of a hormone previously detectable. The one factor we are trying to pinpoint—linear growth—is so intertwined with general growth of the whole body, we must look at several different endocrine glands and their hormones to see how these chemicals affect our height. The diagram (Fig. 5) shows you the approximate location of the pituitary, thyroid, pancreas, adrenals and the gonads (ovaries and testes). All of these endocrine glands produce hormones that play an essential part in linear growth.

How A Body Grows 33

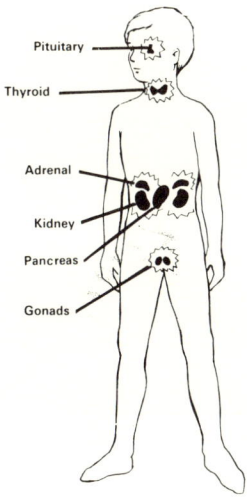

Fig. 5. Location of endocrine glands concerned with human growth (Courtesy of Human Growth Foundation)

PITUITARY GLAND

The pituitary is a pea-sized gland housed in the center of your skull straight back from the top of your nose. For a long time after its presence was discovered, scientists thought it did nothing more important than produce phlegm to lubricate the throat. In fact, in 1543 the tiny structure was named pituitary from the Latin word for mucus. (Our word "spit" has the same origin.) Science has come a long way since then, and now we know that the ten different hormones secreted by the pituitary's two parts, the anterior and posterior lobes, control the growth of bones, muscles and viscera, ovulation and sperm production, the balance of body fluids, and the contraction of uterine muscles during labor, the function of the adrenal and thyroid glands, the metabolism of fat, the development of the mammary glands and secretion of milk, among other things. No wonder the pituitary is known as the "master gland"!

One hormone from the anterior lobe, named somatotrophin, is so essential to tissue growth that it is commonly referred to as the growth hormone, or GH. Most scientific discoveries begin with interesting human stories, and so did the discovery of the pituitary's link with height, which eventually culminated in the isolation of human growth hormone (HGH) in 1956 by Dr. Choh Hao Li at the Hormone Research Laboratory of the University of California in Berkeley, California. The story begins with the hobby of an 18th-century London surgeon, John Hunter, who collected medical specimens. He yearned to add the skeleton of the famous giant of the day, an Irishman named Charles Byrnes, who claimed to be eight feet four inches tall. But Mr. Byrne, who was still very much alive, didn't take kindly to Dr. Hunter's idea, and asked his friends to please encase his coffin in lead after he died and sink it at sea. Well, money can't buy everything but it usually helps, and for 500 pounds, Hunter bribed the undertakers to give the body to him instead of to the sea, and the Irishman's skeleton still hangs on view today in London. But it's not 8'4", it's 7'7", which is still giant sized.

In 1909, 126 years after Byrne's death, the great American neurosurgeon Harvey Cushing examined the giant's skull as part of his study of the pituitary gland. Deformation of the bone surrounding the gland indicated that the pituitary had been considerably enlarged.

Cushing and others went on with further studies that not only proved the link between the pituitary and growth but led to the isolation of the growth hormone itself as well as the discovery that children who are deficient in growth hormone will not grow. In the last two decades scientists have demonstrated that the proper injection of growth hormone will help these deficient children, medically termed hypopituitary dwarfs, to grow. The catch is that only *human* growth hormone works; it's one hormone that is called "species specific." In other words, GH from a cow won't do us a bit of good.

HGH makes us grow taller by somehow facilitating the growth of all cells and the development of our bones. The pituitary produces HGH throughout life. Dr. Salvatore Raiti, Director of the National Pituitary Agency, told me HGH "is needed not only for growth but also for carbohydrate, fat and protein metabolism in all ages." Research concerning how, why, where, and when it works has been a hotbed of inquiry in recent years, and we'll devote a whole chapter to it later.

Three other pituitary hormones that are indirectly related to growth are called trophic, or sustaining, hormones. They control the secretion of hormones in other glands that are more directly involved in human growth. These trophic hormones are:

1. thyrotrophin (TSH), which stimulates the thyroid gland to secrete thyroxine,
2. adrenocorticotrophic hormone (ACTH), which stimulates the adrenal glands to secrete their steroid hormones, especially cortisone,
3. the gonadotrophins (LH & FSH), which control production of sex hormones from the ovaries and testes.

The function of these hormones shows the self-regulating feedback system of some of the endocrine glands. A trophic hormone speeds up production of its target gland. Then some of the hormones thus stimulated send a message back to the pituitary to slow down on its production of the trophic hormone. It's like the thermostat that controls your furnace and keeps the house temperature constant.

In recent years scientists have learned that the master gland has a master, which is the part of the brain to which it's attached, the hypothalamus (see Figure 6).

The blood supply to the pituitary first passes through this mass of nerve tissue, and recent discoveries are proving that chemicals from the hypothalamus control secretion of pituitary hormones. Interestingly enough, the hypothalamus is connected to the brain's center for our highest thought pro-

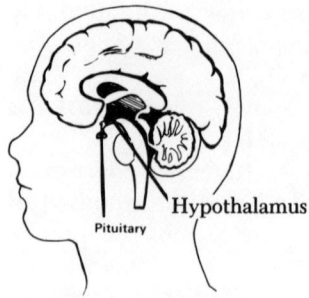

Fig. 6. The pituitary gland is attached to the hypothalamus. (Courtesy of Human Growth Foundation)

cess, the cerebrum. So we may discover that the mind really does have control over the body's most basic operations.

THYROID GLAND

The thyroid gland is a mass of tissue in front of the windpipe and its claim to fame in growth regulation is one of the first hormones to be so identified—thyroxine. Cued by the pituitary, thyroxine alone isn't capable of producing normal growth, but its presence is essential for normal growth to occur. Whereas HGH stimulates an increase in size, the thyroid hormones control the rate of maturation and help reshape the bones to adult form and proportion. Dramatic experiments have shown that tadpoles with the thyroid removed grow to giant-sized tadpoles without becoming frogs, and tadpoles fed extra thyroid become frogs prematurely and are dwarfed.

As Sarah Riedman explains in her excellent book, *Hormones: How They Work,* thyroxin brings about growth by increasing the synthesis of body protein and by enhancing the secretion of HGH. In a child's early years it aids growth by promoting the metabolism of fat from its storage places in the body, and this metabolic process furnishes the energy supply during rapid growth. As the child grows, thyroid hormones help coordinate the proper body proportions during each stage of development, and eventually help to cause the bones to stop growing when the adult maturation level is reached.

Another thyroid hormone has recently been discovered that has a big effect on bone growth. Calcitonin influences the uptake of calcium by bone, as we'll see in the next section when we look at how bones grow. We'll also see how mineralization of bone is affected by parathormone, the hormone secreted by the parathyroid glands, which are four tiny glands paired on either side of the thyroid.

PANCREAS

The pancreas gland is the source of the hormone insulin. Traditionally assigned the role of promoting the transfer of sugar from the blood stream into the cells, insulin is usually brought to mind in reference to diabetes. A diabetic is deficient in insulin and requires injections of the hormone to prevent a potentially lethal sugar build-up in the blood.

In addition to aiding sugar metabolism, scientists have learned, insulin plays an important part in protein synthesis, and therefore in overall body growth. There's a complex relationship between HGH and insulin. Some experiments have shown that when both hormones are absent, treatment with growth hormone alone is not adequate to produce normal growth. As we'll see in a later chapter when we look at the effects of nutrition on growth, protein synthesis affects the size of cells in a growing human body, and a lack of insulin seems to indicate a relationship with very small cells.

Other studies are demonstrating the special importance of insulin to normal growth of the fetus. Insulin may be the primary growth-regulator before birth, more important than growth hormone. A team of pediatric endocrinologists at Children's Hospital in Detroit are currently watching the growth process of a one and a half year old child who was born very small for gestational age, and a lack of insulin was diagnosed at birth. From the first day he has received insulin, but it does not appear that his growth, stunted before birth, will ever catch up to average, even though he is doing well in all other respects. Other babies born of diabetic mothers who have been exposed to extra insulin have not only arrived on the delivery table plump and chubby, but also longer than the average 19- to 21-inch baby.

ADRENAL GLANDS

The two adrenal glands, each an inch or two long, cap the kidneys. The inside part, called the medulla, secretes a hormone you've probably heard of often: adrenalin, the "fight or flight" mechanism that helps a body react to emergencies.

The outer part of the glands, the cortex, secretes a large group of hormones known as corticosteroids. One that's essential to many physiologic functions is cortisone. Treatments of cortisone for some illnesses have shown that when present in excess amounts, it inhibits bone growth. Cortisone is essential to bone formation, but doctors are wary of ordering cortisone therapy unless the adrenals cannot supply normal amounts. Once again we see an example of the splendid balance of our human machinery, and more does not necessarily mean better.

The adrenal cortex also secretes both female and male hormones. Male sex hormones, called androgens, of which testosterone is best known, are excreted mainly by the testes, and the female hormones, estrogen and progestrone, are mostly supplied by the ovaries. But all the sex hormones are also excreted in relatively small amounts by the adrenals.

During puberty the output of adrenal androgens in both boys and girls is radically increased. As explained in the National Institutes of Health's excellent book, *How Children Grow,* scientists have recently learned that these androgens stimulate the adolescent growth spurt, help mature the reproductive system, and also promote the process by which bone growth is ended. Therefore, these hormones wield a double-edged sword to the growing process. They initiate one of the fastest growth periods of the human body, but at the same time they signal the end of the bone growth.

GONADS

Puberty begins when the hypothalamus signals the pituitary to put out increasing levels of two trophic hormones, the gonadotrophins, which are the same in both sexes and stimulate the testes and ovaries to secrete their appropriate sex hormones and to produce sperm and begin ovulation. The changes in the body caused by the action of these hormones in conjunction with growth hormone are enormous, as you well know. The androgens produced in huge supply by the testes supplement and augment the remarkable male adolescent growth begun by the adrenal androgens. In addition to length, the bones grow wider and more developed. Testosterone induces other body growth factors: body hair, muscles, facial changes, penis growth, voice change, etc. The boy begins to look and feel like a man.

The radical change from girl to woman is also caused by these little chemicals, the sex hormones. She develops a softer, rounder form, with wider hips, fuller breasts. Her voice is richer and deeper, her movements more graceful. She shoots up in height too. The ovaries also produce a small amount of male androgen, which supplements the growth action of the adrenal androgen. A girl's rapid growth phase usually begins a couple of years earlier than a boy's, and it doesn't last as long. Estrogen seems to hasten the final ending of bone growth, so females end up shorter than men.

Of all the hormones that are important in the regulation of the growth of our bodies, calcitonin and parathormone (the hormones involved in calcium retention of bone) and insulin are the only ones, so far as is known, which are not under the direct control of the pituitary gland. Next time you look in a mirror, think about that little pea-sized bulb straight back in from your nose.

BONES

We've discussed genes and hormones, and their minuteness makes it difficult to grasp their importance, much less understand how they work. So let's move along to a more obvious factor of our height that we can grab hold of: our bones. Obviously, increase in height is due to a progressive growth of bone. If bones don't grow, the child doesn't grow.

Directions for bone growth are part of the DNA's genetic code, and stimulation of proper bone growth is caused by HGH

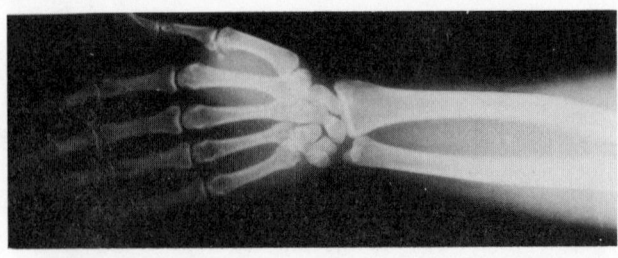
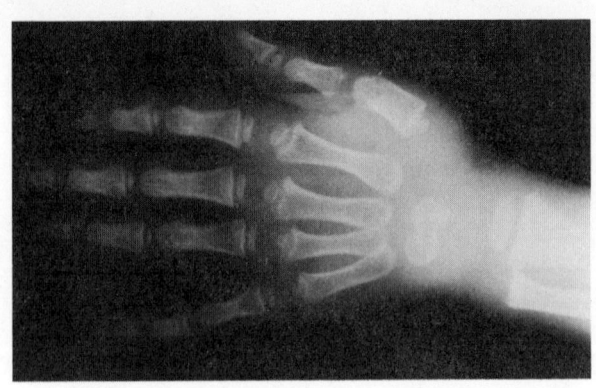
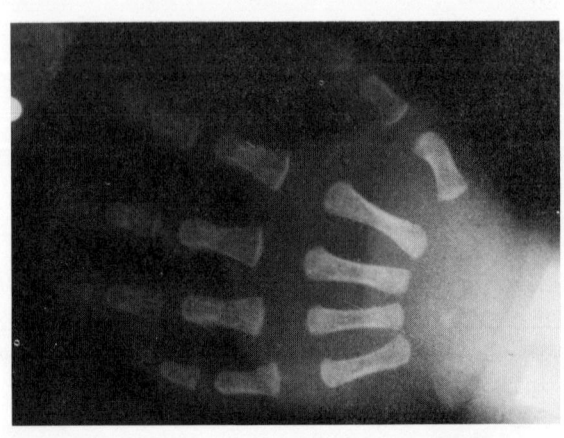

Growth occurs at the ends of the long bones where areas of cartilage (epiphyses) are located. These photographs illustrate the bone formation in the hands of an infant, a five-year-old child and an adult. (Photo courtesy of Human Growth Foundation)

and other hormones. However, even if both of these factors—genes and hormones—are properly present and accounted for, there must also be the correct bone-cell organization and chemical structure for normal growth to occur.

There are three chief ingredients of bones: 1) water (I know that seems strange, but remember that 70% of our whole body is water!); 2) organic material which is mostly a protein matrix called collagen, and 3) minerals, mainly a basic calcium phosphate compound. The skeleton begins in the second month of embryonic life in the form of cartilage, a flexible connective tissue like that in the nose and ears. The process by which cartilage is replaced by true bone is called ossification, and it begins in fetal life, continues through childhood, and the completed process marks the end of puberty. During ossification, bones grow in two directions—length and width. After mature bones are formed and stop growing longer, they can still grow wider.

The NIH book *How Children Grow* gives an excellent description of how bones grow. Cartilage cells arrange themselves in ordered columns and then disintegrate. As they break down, the protein matrix called collagen grows into the space they leave. Collagen is one of the most abundant proteins in the body. Each of its molecules contains almost 3,500 of the amino acid building blocks. This soft but firm protein matrix absorbs minerals from the blood and hard crystals attach to the collagen fibers. The protein fibers give bone its resiliency, and the mineral deposits, which are mainly calcium phosphate, give bone its strength.

The areas in which the conversion of cartilage begins are called primary centers of ossification. Unlike cartilage, they show up on X-rays. These centers of ossification move toward each other until a thin cartilage plate remains between bones and serves as a growth center. As you can see in the sketch (Fig. 7) of a child's thigh bone (femur), for example, the bone is really in three parts as compared to the adult's single bone. In a child, the shaft or diaphysis is separated from each knobby end, the epiphysis, by a cartilage plate. The cartilage cells on

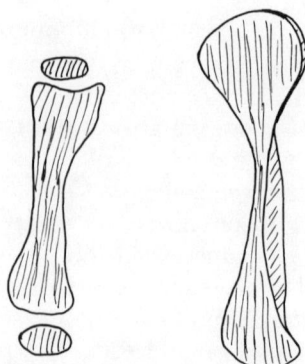

Fig. 7. A child's thigh bone, *left*, and an adult's thigh bone, *right*. The child's bone consists of three sections: 2 epiphyses at top and bottom and the diaphysis, which is the long shaft in the middle. Between each epiphysis and the diaphysis is the cartilage area where new bone-growth occurs. In the adult bone, sex hormones have caused fusion of the epiphyses with the diaphysis, and no further linear growth is possible.

the side next to the epiphysis continue to multiply and on the side of the plate the cartilage cells are converted to bone. In this way the epiphyses are pushed out and the bone grows longer at both ends. Finally, under the direction of adrenal androgens, the cartilage cells in the plate stop multiplying and are replaced by bone. The growth plate disappears and the diaphysis and epiphysis are joined together in what is called the epiphyseal-closure process. After that, further linear growth is impossible.

Bone can be formed directly too, without formation of a cartilage model, and by this process a bone grows wider, changes its shape and maintains a hollow inner core, the marrow cavity, which grows larger as the bone grows. Remember learning about osteoclasts and osteoblasts in biology class and trying to remember which was which? Well, osteoBLASTS are the bone cells that BLAST new bone into shape, and osteoCLASTS are the bone cells that CRASH and destroy old bone. (How's that for a memory tool?) By this ingenious process, new bone is deposited on the outer surface and simultaneously old bone is resorbed from the center. The hollow center makes the bones light so we don't drag around solid tons of calcium phosphate, and it also provides a nice safe place for bone marrow, from which red cells of the blood are produced.

Bones of the body don't all grow at the same rate. The skull grows slowly, the bones of the trunk a little faster, and the bones of the arms and legs faster still. As the body grows, it changes in proportion. Under the influence of the thyroid and sex hormones, the body matures as it grows up. Before puberty the legs grow faster than the trunk, but during the adolescent growth spurt most of the height gain results from growth of the trunk.

Exercise of the body makes bone-building cells more active, so athletes usually have more bone as well as muscle than the average individual. Your bones will get stronger and thicker if you do a lot of heavy work or exercise, even after you are an adult.

The process of mineralization of bone is essential to our growth, and so is the reverse process of demineralization. The basic raw materials for bone growth are protein, calcium, phosphorus, and vitamin D. The vitamin helps the body absorb calcium and phosphorus in the intestines so the blood can carry them to the bones.

But calcium and phosphorus are important not just as the basic mineral component of bone. They are also essential in other workings of the body. As we learned earlier, phosphorus is a key ingredient of DNA and RNA and therefore basic to life. An exact level of calcium in the blood controls behavior of the nerves, which carry messages to the muscles. When the calcium level falls too low, muscles will contract suddenly and violently. When the serum calcium rises too high, the action of the nerves becomes sluggish and the person becomes drowsy and irritable. If the high level is continued long, the result is loss of consciousness and death. The serum calcium level also affects the heart's ability to beat at the proper rate and force.

Calcium and phosphorus levels in the blood are so vital that if you don't eat foods that supply enough of these minerals, your body will dissolve what it needs from the supply in your bones and teeth.

In his interesting story of bone, *The Armor Within Us,* Joseph Samachson explains that calcium is maintained in the blood at a remarkably steady level of about ten milligrams in a hundred milliliters, or what scientists refer to as ten milligram percent. The phosphorus level is close to three and a half or four milligram percent. These slight traces, so vital to life, are controlled partly by two hormones we discussed earlier. Calcitonin, secreted by the thyroid gland, is stimulated by an increase in calcium level in the blood and promotes the uptake of calcium by the osteoblasts. When the blood calcium level is reduced to normal, the calcitonin production shuts down. On the other hand, a fall of blood calcium level encourages parathormone excretion from the parathyroid glands, and this hormone promotes the action of the osteoclasts and the calcium flow from bone back into the bloodstream.

The phosphorus levels in the blood are under delicate controls also. The interaction between these minerals, blood levels and bone also includes the kidneys, which exert control by the amount of minerals they extract from the blood and eliminate through the urine. The whole mechanism is amazingly delicate and is another example of how intimately interwoven are all parts of the body. In studying our bones' linear growth, it's important to realize that malfunction in any of these interwoven parts of the balancing mechanism can have profound effect on the development of bone and therefore on the entire growth process. If there is interference with either the process of bone formation or bone resorption, bone growth is abnormal.

I feel that we've barely peeked through the door at the complicated process of how a body grows. But if you understand generally how the action of genes, hormones and bones determine how tall you are, then you will be better prepared to understand why some of us are short and what can go wrong with the growing-up process.

So far we've only discussed some internal, biological factors, and later we must consider some of the external, environmental factors that affect growth. Scientists still engage in a big "nature vs. nurture" controversy over which factors influence a human's development more, heredity or environment. They both play a vital role in determining how tall we are. Food, exercise, sleep, our emotions, and even what we're thinking about all affect our height. As Alice said, the whole story sure gets "curiouser and curiouser."

3 Should You Worry About Your Child's Height?

A hair perhaps divides the false and true;
And upon what, prithee, may life depend?
Omar Khayyam

While I was waiting for a meeting of the local Human Growth Foundation chapter to begin, I glanced at a recent newspaper article on display. It told about a son of a HGF member: "Doug is 11 years old and stands just a little taller than his three-year-old brother." Doug came over and looked at the article too. "You see that 'little'?" he said. "Little can mean a lot of different things! Some people might read this and think I'm just a half an inch taller than my brother, but I'm a whole lot bigger than he is!"

Every inch is important to a child's growth, and you, as a parent, should be aware of how many and how fast those inches are piling up.

The most obvious reason to be aware of your child's height is because "growth is, in itself, a reflection of life," as pediatrician Alvin Hayles of the Mayo Clinic phrased it. Another pediatric specialist, Dr. Louis Underwood at the University of North Carolina, sees growth as "one of the best readouts a physician has as to disease of any kind." In an interview with *Medical World News,* Dr. Underwood urged careful measurement of every child to follow the rate of linear (upward) growth. "Just as tree rings testify to past wet and dry seasons, spurts and lags of stature are evidence of early insults, such as recurring infection, poor nutrition, social upheaval." But many physicians who routinely take pulse and blood pressure "completely miss the good diagnostic tool of charting linear growth patterns." Short stature is not itself a diagnosis of a specific condition, but rather a sign or symptom.

There are many ways for parents to be aware if their children are growing properly. One is to compare him or her in height and overall physical ability and endurance with friends the same age. Another growth guide is how fast the child outgrows clothes. Too often I hear parents complain, "I just bought you new pants three months ago—they can't be too short already!" Little do these parents know how much more costly in money, time and anguish it would be for them if their child wasn't outgrowing his pants so rapidly.

The method of judging growth that usually jumps to mind is measuring.

"How tall is Johnny?"

"Let's measure and see."

Sounds simple, but is it? What's the best way to do it? How do you relate that mark on the wall to the child's age, his past growth, his future growth? How do you know what height is "right"? Isn't this a problem that should be left up to the doctor, like listening to heart beat? Well, let's look at some answers to questions about measuring height.

WHO SHOULD DO THE MEASURING?

It seems that the customary practice in this country is for children to be measured in weight and length quite regularly by the family doctor or pediatrician while the children are infants and up to about age two or three. After that the checkup intervals stretch out until, by adolescence, many children are seen by a doctor only when and if an illness is serious enough to warrant a visit. It has been my experience in five different states I've lived in that schools do not require a physical every year. Sometimes students are measured at elementary schools. When I was room mother for my daughter Cathy's sixth grade class, I was in charge of "weighing and measuring" . . . and I hope no one considered the results very professional as I found it very difficult to work the darned scale. By the way, that's when I discovered I was exactly average in both height and weight for a sixth grader.

As Dr. Underwood and other growth specialists have pointed out, many doctors do not pay much attention to measuring height. So ask yourself a very important question. Do I take my child (or baby or teenager) to a doctor at least once a year for a physical that includes measuring height? If the answer is yes to that question, then ask: Who does the measuring, the nurse or the doctor? Does the doctor keep a growth chart on my child that shows the rate of growth compared to the average growth rate? Have I seen this growth chart and do I understand it? Do I feel certain from the explanations and comments that the doctor has given me that my child's growth is being carefully measured and analyzed for abnormalities? If the answers to these questions completely reassure you that your child's doctor is taking good care of following your child's growth pattern from birth to adulthood, then your answer to "who should measure?" will be "the doctor." But if you don't feel secure about that answer, for whatever reason, then there's an alternative: *you,* the parent—good old Mom and Dad.

WHAT'S THE BEST WAY TO MEASURE HEIGHT?

One of the medical advisors for the Human Growth Foundation is Dr. William Hoffman, a pediatric endocrinologist at Children's Hospital of Michigan. When I asked him about the right way to measure, he said, "The person's heels, knees, buttocks, shoulders and back of the head should be against a flat surface perpendicular to the floor with the chin parallel to the floor." When I asked about the scales in most doctors' offices on which the child stands and faces the inch gauge and the metal bar swings up and over the head, he made a face and shook his head. There is no way to assure proper posture on that wobbly platform with no vertical plane supporting the body . . . and the crosspiece is rarely at an exact right angle.

Pediatrician James M. Tanner of the University of London

Accurate measurements are essential in determining growth patterns. (Photo courtesy of Human Growth Foundation)

Should You Worry About Your Child's Height?

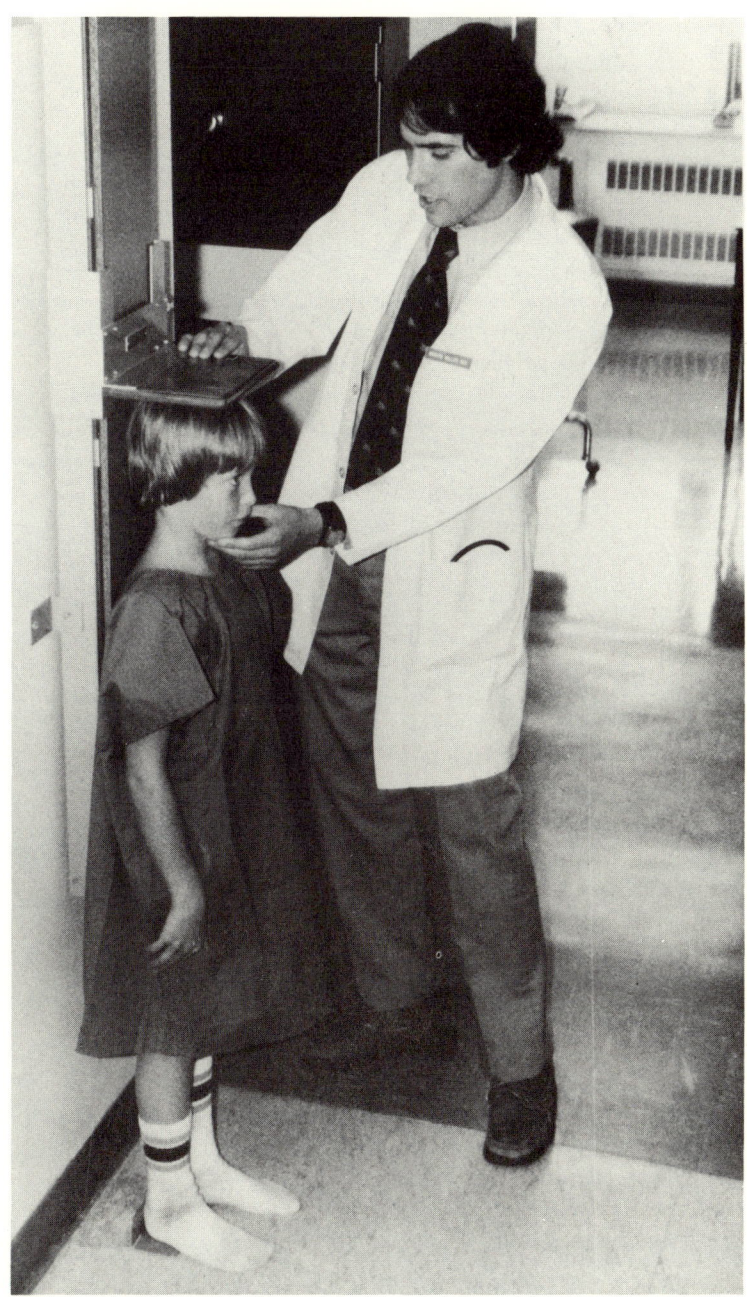

Institute of Child Health and an acknowledged world authority on child growth patterns has designed a "stadiometer." It's a simple device consisting of a vertical panel, a horizontal head block that slides up and down like a sash window, and a small dial that reads out height to the nearest millimeter. Many American pediatricians are importing this instrument, but you can set up a similar, homemade apparatus for measuring a standing person. All you need is:

1. A smooth wall at a true right angle to the floor (be careful of baseboards—they'll destroy your right angle. Sometimes the side of a refrigerator will do.)
2. A measuring guide marked in inches and/or centimeters (Let me warn you here that to have true communication with your doctor, you'd better use the metric system—he's been thinking in centimeters for years.)
3. A head block, such as a thick book, that you can hold firmly level across the head at a right angle to the wall

Then have your child stand in an "at attention" posture with heels, buttocks, shoulders and head firmly against the wall. Dr. Frank Falkner of the Fels Research Institute in Yellow Springs, Ohio, a major growth research center, advises a person being measured to "make yourself as tall as you can, but keep your heels on the floor." Dr. Falkner explains that "this conscious effort to stretch up stretches the joint spaces to provide a reproducible stance." Holding the chin parallel with the floor will also minimize variations between measuring stances. Did you know that everyone's taller in the morning? A tall child may well be a half inch taller early in the day. Later on our joints all compress a little, but this difference won't matter if we "stand tall" when being measured.

Dr. Hoffman recommends measuring a child's height at six-month intervals. If you do, you will probably notice that your child grows fastest in the spring and summer. Scientists have determined that season has a definite influence on growth, and in the northern hemisphere height gains are greatest in April, May and June and least during September, October and November. The opposite holds true for weight gain, which may be five or six times as great in the fall as in the spring. As far as I've been able to determine, the reason for these seasonal variations is still unknown.

Pick a time of the year that you will easily remember, such as the child's birthday and his half-birthday, or Christmas and the Fourth of July, and then measure on a consistent schedule year after year. But take some advice from a short person: don't make a big deal out of this measuring ceremony. Do it consistently and accurately, but don't fuss over it so the child will feel it's his or her personal failure if he hasn't grown much. Frankly, I always hated to find out how much I didn't grow. Remember that you are measuring height as an indicator of health to help you determine if there's any need for concern. Growing is hardly the same sort of activity as playing baseball or singing in the school play and does not deserve either applause or boos. Also, any child who's a slow grower does not like to have that chart tacked or marked permanently on the wall for all the world to see his nongrowth. So maybe you should use the inside of a closet!

Part and parcel of measuring your child should be to record the measurement on a growth chart, available from your doctor or the Human Growth Foundation (see Figures 8 and 9). Marked on each standard growth chart is the average growth rate, so marking your child's height opposite the correct age and number of inches or centimeters will show you how your child compares to average. But more importantly, when you connect the marks from one year to the next, it will show you the *rate* of growth. Comparing this resultant line to the standard growth curve can be a far more important indicator of concern than the specific height at any one age. But before you get into interpreting the readings of your child's particular chart, we'd better understand a little more about the average growth rate.

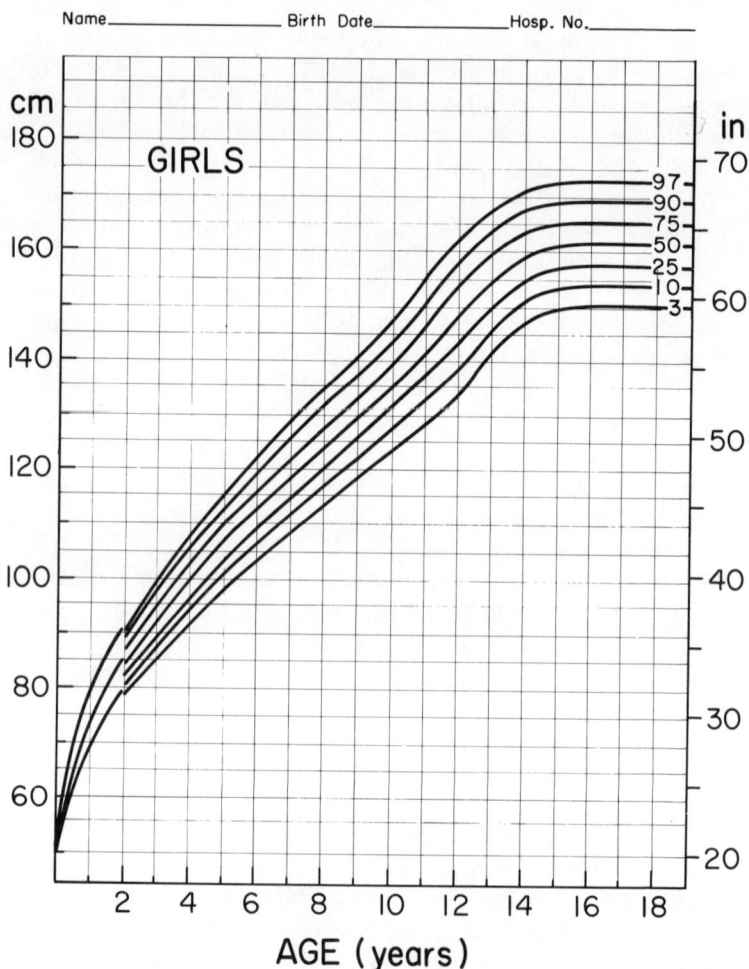

Fig. 8. Growth Chart for Girls. This chart and the Growth Chart for Boys (Fig. 9) show the average growth curve for Caucasions by using percentile lines. The 50th percentile indicates that 50% of the population are shorter than that line. The 3rd-percentile line means that only 3% are shorter, and most doctors think that anyone measuring below the 3rd percentile should be examined for growth problems. A normal growth curve should follow the same smooth pattern as these lines.

Should You Worry About Your Child's Height? 53

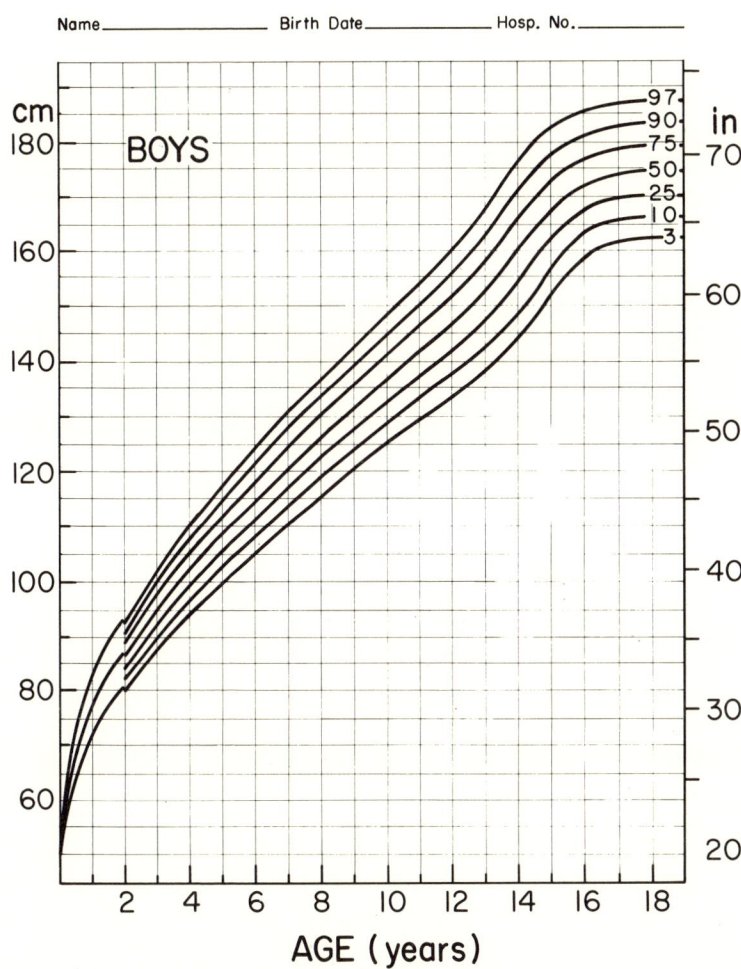

Fig. 9. Growth Chart for Boys. (See Figure 8 for Girls.) (Growth charts courtesy of Children's Hospital of Michigan, based on data from J. M. Tanner, 1966.)

WHAT IS THE AVERAGE GROWTH RATE?

One of the most important things to remember when you study an average-growth-rate chart is the wide height-variation in children of the same age. The center line, or the 50-percentile line means that there are 50 percent below and 50 percent above that line. Therefore, by the very nature of these charts, somebody must be way below and somebody way above this center line.

It's very difficult for growth researchers to obtain an accurate average growth rate for several reasons. When they measure many children of different ages, and figure the average height for each age, this is called a cross-sectional study, and it's useful in comparing groups. The average size of eight-year-olds in New York City public schools can be compared with the average size of eight-year-olds in a Japanese school or a French school. But these studies do not show how a child grows from ages 6 to 8, for example, because the same children aren't measured at different ages. A growth curve based on cross-sectional studies does not show anyone actually growing.

When the growth of the same group of children is followed over a period of time it's called a longitudinal study, and it's a much more difficult study to conduct. It takes years to complete while the investigator waits for the subjects to grow up, families move about, and the whole project can become very expensive.

The results of the HEW growth study I mentioned earlier were announced by the National Center for Health Statistics in 1976. The study was based on 20,000 U.S. children over a period of 15 years, and excellent charts made from these statistics are available now from the government and HGF. Many other research centers are conducting growth studies. The work at Fels Research Institute is well known because it was written up and photographed so beautifully in the Life Science Library's volume, *Growth.* At Fels more than 800 children born since 1929 have been serially and scientifically measured, X-

Should You Worry About Your Child's Height?

rayed and tested in a search to define the basic principles of growth.

The average growth charts all show the rapid growth in infancy, the slowing down during childhood, and the last big push during puberty. The most rapid and crucial period of growth doesn't even show on the charts because it occurs in the 9 months before birth. Slow linear growth at this stage can have a lasting effect, as we'll see later.

The curve through infancy is the supine or lying-down length. (And don't babies always hate being measured?) As you follow the center line on either the boy's or girl's chart you see that it follows, approximately, Dr. Blizzard's rule of thumb, mentioned in the previous chapter: 10 inches the first year, 5 inches the second, and about 2½ inches every year thereafter until puberty. It's this last growth spurt at puberty that varies so widely between boys and girls, between different ages, and between number of inches gained. As you can see in both the boy's and girl's charts, the older the ages the more widespread the variation in the normal growth curve.

The proportions of the body grow at different rates during this adolescent growth spurt. As explained in the NIH booklet *How Children Grow,* feet and hands increase first, then calves and forearms, hips and chest, and the shoulders reach mature growth last. The overall increase in height during adolescence is due more to the lengthening of the trunk rather than the legs.

There may be a variation of four years between the beginning of puberty in one normal child and another. In the U.S. the typical girl now starts this phase at 10½, according to the NIH. For the next 2½ years she grows at the rate of about 3 inches per year. The menstrual cycle begins at the average age of 13, and then there is a rapid decline in linear growth. By age 16 her epiphyses are usually closed and further growth is impossible.

The average American boy begins his adolescence at age 13 and has a longer, more intense growth spurt. For at least the next 2½ years he shoots up at the rate of 4 inches a year, equalling the dramatic growth of a two-year-old. Usually a male's epiphyses don't close until his late teens.

These wide differences in male and female average growth rates during adolescence are hard to pinpoint on a chart, but the age at which this maturation begins determines to a large degree what the ultimate adult height will be. The further advanced a child is in sexual maturation the less growth potential he retains. Taller, more mature children usually stop growing sooner and sometimes end up shorter than their more immature, smaller friends.

The differences between the sexual maturation and growth rates of boys and girls was presented by Dr. Tanner in his interesting article in *Scientific American,* "Growing Up." The charts showing the sequence of events of puberty of both sexes are reprinted from that article. Note that the start of the menstrual cycle is a late event in female puberty and usually comes after the peak of the growth spurt is over. The most easily detectable sign in both sexes of beginning puberty is the appearance of pubic hair.

When you are comparing your child's growth rate to an average growth rate, it's important for you to understand the tremendous variation of this adolescent growth spurt and its influence on your child's ultimate height.

Notice also on the average growth charts (Figures 8 and 9) that the line flows smoothly. As Dr. Tanner points out, "Human growth is a regular process . . . it does not proceed by fits and starts." In fact, this constant tempo or velocity of growth is the most reliable indicator of how your child is doing as to growth. By the time your child is 3, his or her growth curve should follow along almost parallel to the average curve of human growth, whether shorter or taller. How far it deviates from the mean or 50-percentile line is referred to by doctors in terms of "standard deviations," which gets into some fairly complicated statistical concepts. For us short people, the growth line we're concerned with is the 3rd percentile, which doctors also refer to as two standard deviations below the mean. Third percentile means that only three percent of the

Should You Worry About Your Child's Height? 57

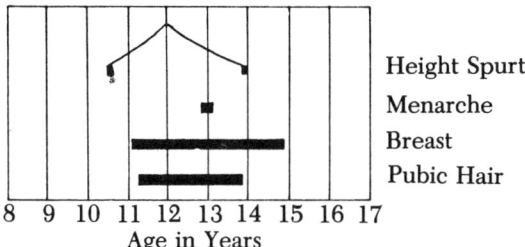

Fig. 10. Sequence of Events of Puberty in Girls at various ages is diagrammed for the average child. The hump in the bar labeled "Height Spurt" represents the peak velocity of the spurt. The bars represent the beginning and completion of the events of puberty. Although the adolescent growth spurt for girls typically begins at age 10.5 and ends at age 14, it can start as early as age 9.5 and end as late as age 15. Similarly, menarche (the onset of menstruation) can come at any time between the ages of 10 and 16.5 and tends to be a late event of puberty. Some girls begin to show breast development as early as age 8 and have completed it by age 13; others may not begin it until age 13 and complete it at age 18. First pubic hair appears after the beginning of breast development in two-thirds of all girls.

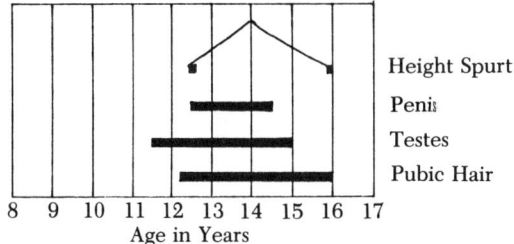

Fig. 11. Sequence of Events of Puberty in Boys is also shown at various ages for the average child. The adolescent growth spurt of boys can begin as early as age 10.5 or as late as age 16 and can end anywhere from age 13.5 to age 17.5. Elongation of the penis can begin from age 10.5 to 14.5 and can end from age 12.5 to 16.5. Growth of the testes can begin as early as age 9.5 or as late as age 13.5 and end at any time between the ages 13.5 and 17. (From "Growing Up" by J. M. Tanner. Copyright (c) September 1973 by Scientific American, Inc. All rights reserved.)

population are shorter, and most physicians think that children that short should be observed closely and possibily have some extra tests to see if abnormalities are present that can be treated.

Sooner or later in any discussion of average growth rates the fact is pointed out that our average height is increasing. According to the NIH, average young adults of today measure one inch more than their parents and two inches taller than their grandparents. As Dr. Tanner points out in "Growing Up," average growth of an entire population is very sensitive to malnutrition and other environmental upsets. As the environmental and social conditions of a country improve, the children not only grow taller but mature faster, and the variation between individuals in different social classes becomes less. During the last century in the industrialized nations of the world, the lower classes are catching up and growing taller faster than the upper classes. The impetus of growth from the more disadvantaged children has pushed up the average growth rate. This process is termed the secular trend of growth and virtually every country in the world seems to have been affected by it. In the last 100 years babies have been heavier and longer at birth. The records show that between 1880 and 1950, the average height of American and Western European children between the ages of five and seven increased more than a half inch every 10 years for a total of four inches. The increase in adolescent height was even more dramatic—seven inches.

Most researchers attribute the secular trends to better medical care and nutrition, especially in infancy. However, Dr. Tanner and others point out that there is a danger in many countries now of children being overfed, and that overfeeding in childhood may be cutting down on our longevity potential. We'll get into the effects of childhood obesity on height in chapter 5, when we cover nutrition in more detail.

Along with increasing height, the average person is also maturing at an earlier age. Life Science Library's *Growth* states, "Early in the century, most men reached their final height at around 26 years; since then the age has dropped to 18 or 19." Also, "In almost every country for which figures are available over the past century, the girls of each generation have been reaching puberty nearly 10 months earlier than their mothers. At the same time, the menopause has been arriving later, so that women's span of fertility has been increasing."

How long can this increase in height and decrease in pubertal age go on? No one knows for sure, but scientists suspect that the increase is leveling off and that we've about reached the maximum average height allowed by the human genetic potential. Tanner notes that the trend has nearly ceased in American and British populations that are economically well-off. Evidently there is an undefined point in our human linear growth pattern at which bigger is definitely not better, and our evolving genes say, "Whoa—stop here." Poor Robert Wadloe, the world's tallest man at 8′11¾″, had such long legs that he didn't have any feeling below his ankles. He died at age 22 of infection resulting from the chafing of his ankle by an iron brace worn to help support his weight of almost 500 pounds.

So, you might ask, if people are growing so much taller why am I still so short? Because the wide range of heights has been unaffected over the years. The *average* has increased, but there are always big and little children, big and little adults. Although big and little alike are all a little bigger than they used to be, there still must be many of us genetically short shrimpos who hold up the bottom line of the growth charts.

HOW INTERPRET YOUR CHILD'S GROWTH CHART?

The key here is steady growth, paralleling the normal growth curve. No peaks and valleys. No plateaus. Your seven-year-old may be tall for his or her age, stop growing for a year and still not look out of place with his classmates, and you might think everything's A-OK. But it's not. As Dr. Blizzard emphasizes, "The *minimum* normal acceptable growth rate between 3 and 12 years of age is 2 inches per year."

DOES YOUR CHILD'S HEIGHT MEASURE UP?

Human Growth Foundation, Inc. is a voluntary, non-profit organization dedicated to helping medical science better understand the process of growth, particularly dwarfism. It is composed of parents and friends of children with growth retardation problems, individuals with short stature, and interested physicians. HGF puts out many excellent brochures that give advice to parents who are concerned about their children's growth. The following are HGF's guidelines to help parents answer the question, "Does your child measure up?"

1. Is he the shortest in his class?
2. Is he still wearing last year's clothes?
3. Is he unable to keep up with the other kids his age at play?
4. Is he growing less than 2 inches per year?

HGF recommends that if you have four "yes" answers, you should suspect a growth problem and consult your pediatrician.

I'd like to add a fifth question for you to consider: Is he complaining that he is too short? In other words, is your child's height bothering him? If his or her classmates are teasing with the usual "runt," "shrimp," "peewee," "squirt," or "shorty," and if the child is worried about it, then you should share his concern.

These guidelines are fine for the years 3 to 12, but what about before and after? I assume that anyone reading this book is already concerned enough about growth that taking a baby under 3 to a doctor for physical check-ups is routine. Measuring height is usually standard practice at that age, so any problems should be detected early.

Around age 12 we get into the touchy stage. How do you know when your child should start the adolescent growth spurt? How do you know if he's just a late maturer or if something's wrong with his development? Dr. Hoffman recommends that if by the end of 8th grade a boy or girl shows no signs whatever of beginning sexual maturation, he or she should be seen by the family physician or pediatrician. Remember that a girl's onset of menstruation does not occur at the start of sexual development. The first indication in a female is usually budding breasts or underarm and pubic hair growth. Your son's testicular growth will not be as obvious to you as your daughter's breasts, but the first fuzzy facial hair is a good clue as well as the changing pitch of his voice.

If either you or your child is concerned about height at any stage of growth, then go to your doctor. To provide support and understanding for your problems is part of his job, and concern with growth patterns has become more prevalent. As reported in *Medical World News,* pediatric endocrinologist Virginia Weldon of St. Louis Children's Hospital has observed that, "More parents than ever before are worrying about their children's stature. Forty years ago, they expected a certain number of their offspring to die of polio or pneumonia, but in our day and age parental expectations rarely if ever include death of a child. Therefore, I think parents worry more about other aspects of development."

What if your doctor gives the, "Don't worry, he'll grow" brush-off? Well, unfortunately this happens often. Part of the problem is that worry over a child's height is a double-edged sword. Yes, it's important to be concerned enough to give the short child any medical therapy he may require and to give him the psychological support to cope with the stigma of being short. On the other hand, if a parent or doctor goes overboard emphasizing worry and concern over a child's failure to grow, it can develop into a real hang-up for the child. As I'll discuss later, if a person is constantly aware that he's short it can hamper his ability to grow in other ways. "I can't play the violin, I'm too short," may sound silly, but that's how the creeping disease of being short can invade the corners of a person's mind. Doctors recognize this potential problem, so they don't want to stir up any unnecessary concern. Besides, the comment, "He'll shoot up overnight," often comes true.

If you feel your doctor isn't answering your questions adequately, perhaps it will help if you make a private appointment and discuss the situation with him away from your child's listening ears.

If your doctor does not allay your fears, if he does not provide further growth testing and evaluation himself, and if he does not refer you to a growth specialist (usually a pediatric endocrinologist, which means a specialist in children's hormone systems), then you can take your child to a specialist on your own. Most major hospitals have them. If you want a specific name to call for an appointment, you can consult with the Human Growth Foundation (see appendix). HGF keeps an up-to-date listing of growth specialists and medical advisors on short stature all over the country.

Following is a list of items of information that a doctor may ask you for in order to evaluate the growth progress of your child. Sometimes these are hard to remember on the spur of the moment, so it's helpful if you jot them down in your own fashion before you go to the doctor's office. The doctor is looking for as complete a picture as possible of the child's growth.

1. All previous records of child's height from other doctors, baby books, school records, or the chart on the wall at home, and be sure to look up the exact birth weight and length.
2. Information about your pregnancy and delivery: for example, were there any complications such as bleeding or infection, were hormones, pills or shots received during pregnancy and if so, during which trimester (first 3 months, middle three months, final 3 months), was labor induced, was the baby born early, was there any problem getting breathing started, any complications in the nursery, did the doctor or nurse mention anything unusual, etc.
3. Milestones in your child's physical and mental development, such as when he first sat up, crawled, walked, rode a tricycle, teeth appeared, when he first talked and was vocabulary and sentence development advanced or be-

hind others of same age, did these milestones occur sooner or later than brothers and sisters.
4. Information regarding child's present health and any signs of symptoms indicating malfunction, including eyes, ears, nose, throat, heart, lungs, digestive tract, bones and muscles, frequency of urination.
5. Information on growth patterns and significant medical history of immediate family (brothers, sisters, parents and grandparents) and if there have been any diseases or problems, such as extremely short stature, failure to enter adolescent development at a reasonable age, diabetes, high blood pressure, unusually tall stature, physical abnormalities, etc.
6. If the child is undergoing adolescent development now, is he or she at about the same stage as classmates? Remember approximate dates when older brothers and sisters entered puberty (girls: breast development and pubic hair; boys: testicular growth, body hair, voice change).

Testing Procedures

In addition to a general physical there are a few tests a doctor may perform to help him determine the cause of growth disturbance. Maybe it will help you to relax and to soothe your child's apprehensions if you know a little about some of these possible tests.

Many different tests of body function require urine and blood samples. Maybe he'll need urine specimens collected over a 24 hour period or perhaps first thing in the morning. The blood sample will be taken from the arm.

The medical history and a physical are the crucial parts of the initial visit. Perhaps the physician will also want lab tests and X-rays to determine the stage of bone development, which is called bone age. Did you know that your child's age can be determined three different ways? His chronological age is the age we commonly refer to, which is the number of years since birth. When talking about stature, the height age is what the average height of the average normal child at a certain age would be. For example, the average 4-year-old is about 40 inches tall, so any child who is 40 inches has a height age of 4 years. The chronological and height ages may or may not be the same.

Bone age or biological age is a third designation, and perhaps the most important one from the physician's point of view. As we learned in the previous chapter, as bones grow more calcium is deposited at the epiphyses. X-rays of bones of the hand and wrists are usually used for this study, and by comparing your child's X-rays to an official standard, radiologists can judge the rate of growth of the bones. If the bones are growing in a normal, average manner, the bone age and chronological age will be the same. If the child is a slow grower, his bones may be growing slowly too. If so, his bone age would be lower than his chronological age.

Bone age is an important tool for indicating how much potential for further growth is still present in the bones. Once the epiphyses have closed, taller growth is impossible.

In addition to extent of bone growth, wrist and hand X-rays are also examined for abnormal growth. Other X-rays are sometimes taken to diagnose growth problems if indicated, such as skull X-rays to determine size and condition of the pituitary gland, or knee X-rays to study possible bone disease or cartilage abnormalities.

Perhaps your child's growth-hormone level will need to be tested, which can be done in different ways, all based on blood samples. These tests can be lengthy and may even involve a short stay in the hospital so the patient can be closely watched. One frequently used HGH test is called the arginine-insulin tolerance test, which takes about two and a half hours and determines the ability of the pituitary gland to secrete growth hormone. As Dr. Hoffman explained the procedure to me, the patient fasts after the evening meal the night before the test, and an IV is started in the arm early the next morning. Two blood samples are taken 15 minutes apart, and then arginine solution (one of the basic amino acids) is infused into the blood. Arginine directly affects the pituitary gland and usually increases the production of HGH. Three additional blood samples are withdrawn at 15-minute intervals and HGH levels determined. Then the hormone insulin is infused into the blood. Insulin lowers the blood sugar level, which in turn normally stimulates HGH secretion. Several blood samples are taken at 15-minute intervals to test the pituitary's response to this stimulation. Both arginine and insulin are used because researchers have found that although a normal pituitary may not respond very well to one of them, 80% of children with normal HGH levels will show an active response to either insulin or arginine infusion.

Growth hormone secretion is also frequently tested by measuring blood levels before and after vigorous exercise, as exercise usually stimulates the release of HGH into the bloodstream.

These tests, or others, may be done in the hospital because the child may not feel well for a while afterwards.

Since growth before birth is a vital influence on the person's ultimate height, what about testing procedures before birth? Pathologist Eugene Perrin recommends that a pregnant woman's initial physical and each subsequent check-up should include measurement of the uterus. By this relatively simple means, the approximate growth of the baby can be followed and any unusual growth failure detected. If growth is slow, perhaps amniocentesis is indicated. In this testing process the doctor withdraws, through the mother's abdomen, some of the fluid surrounding the fetus. Analysis of this fluid can detect if certain birth defects are developing within the fetus, some of which can be corrected by proper treatment of the mother. The test was developed as a research technique, but it is now widely used clinically as a diagnostic procedure.

By the way, when you are discussing your child's growth with the doctor, be prepared for one possible communication block: the metric system. Physicians and scientists think and talk in metric terms, and if you're saying inches and he's saying centimeters you may leave his office more confused than when you went in. Personally, I'm finding it very hard to convert, but I'm trying. Until I get the hang of it, I'm not too bashful or embarrassed to say, "What do you mean in inches?"

HEIGHT PREDICTION

When you talk with the doctor about your child's height, one of the questions on your mind may be, "How tall will he grow?" The old guide of approximately twice the height at age two is still true. However, your doctor may be able to use a new tool for predicting adult height in children prepared by Dr. Alex Roche, Dr. Howard Wainer and David Thissen (hence called the RWT height-prediction method).

Four pieces of information are used: length of child measured while he's lying down (which is about 1.25 cm longer than standing height), present weight, average height of parents, and bone age of hand-wrist. These four values are then compared with a set of master tables to compute the prediction. The program is based on growth studies at Fels Research Institute.

According to Dr. Wainer, predictions are most accurate for children between the ages of two and twelve. The estimates fall within two inches of actual adult height 90% of the time, and within one inch half the time. As long as your son is under 16 or daughter under 14, the system will work. Dr. Wainer adds that, "Hundreds of doctors have written for copies of the computer program to do RWT prediction." It can be obtained through him at the Bureau of Social Science Research in Washington, D.C., or through Dr. Roche at Fels. Dr. Wainer believes that it is a simple, inexpensive and accurate way to check for growth problems while there is still time to do something about them. As Dr. Roche explains, growth charts tell the past and present, but not the future. "Accurate predictions of adult stature would greatly assist the management of short or tall children and those children receiving hormones or other therapeutic substances that can influence the rates of elongation and maturation of the skeleton."

Should You Worry About Your Child's Height? 67

Most Frequent Causes of Short Stature

We've discussed how you as a parent can follow your child's growth and what danger signals should alert you to growth problems. Then we went to the doctor's office to see what information and tools he uses to evaluate your child's growth pattern. Now we're ready for the diagnosis, so here's a list of the most frequent causes of short stature. Some we'll discuss in greater depth in later chapters.

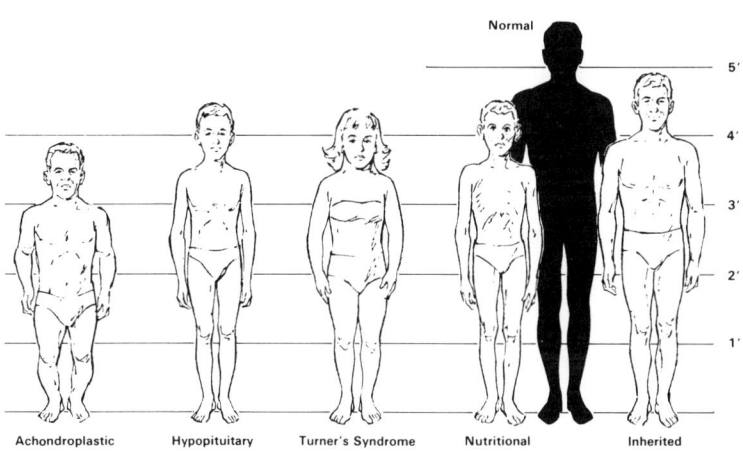

Fig. 12. A comparison of 18-year-old dwarfs with a normal person of the same age shown by the shaded figure. (Courtesy of Human Growth Foundation)

1. GENETIC OR FAMILIAL SHORT STATURE

Short parents tend to produce short offspring, and this is the most common cause of short stature in the United States. My mother and father were 4'11" and 5'7". My brother is 5'7", my sister 5 feet, and I'm 4'9". We are a typical short family. There is nothing wrong with our hormone production, bone growth, body proportions or anything else. The reason we are small is embedded in the genetic structure of our DNA, which dictates the response to the stimulation of the growth hormone. We don't produce less growth hormone than a family of six-footers, nor have we been adversely affected by bad health, poor nutrition or other unfavorable environmental influences.

Genetically short children grow at a constant rate each year. Their growth curves lie parallel to, but below the average percentile lines, and their bone ages usually correspond to their chronological ages.

Treatment of problems caused by genetic short stature fall in the realm of psychological support, which we'll discuss at length in later chapters.

2. CONSTITUTIONAL DELAYED GROWTH WITH DELAYED ADOLESCENCE

This type of growth pattern falls within the "unusual but normal" category and is one of the most frequent causes of short stature that are of concern to children, parents and doctors. As explained in the Human Growth Foundation's booklet, "Patterns of Growth," prepared by medical advisors Dr. Robert Blizzard and Dr. Henry Sauls, approximately ten times as many boys as girls are affected. The child is shorter than average for most of his life and also enters the adolescent growth phase late. A boy at age ten will be about the size of a seven-year-old, and his bone maturation will be that of a seven-year-old. A year later at age eleven, both his height and bone age will be that of an eight-year-old.

Usually these children have been behind their agemates since preschool years, although occasionally this pattern of delayed growth doesn't begin until age ten or even later. They continue to grow at a slow but normal rate. When they finally reach adolescence, which may begin two, three, or four years later than in most of their friends, they have a normal growthspurt and usually end up as tall as their parents.

This pattern of growth is strongly influenced by the parents. If a father grew slowly and matured late, chances are his son will too. Normally it is mainly our heredity, not environment, that paces the change of puberty.

Should You Worry About Your Child's Height? 69

Four 14-year-old boys showing comparable size of boy with constitutional delayed growth with delayed adolescence. (Photo courtesy of Human Growth Foundation)

Growth studies in recent years are lending clinical proof to traditional observations that short adolescents continue growing for more years than tall adolescents. NIH research scientists note that: "The tall girl will usually grow only a little taller; the height of the short boy can in time exceed that of his tallest friends. Such information can be of great help in reassuring and allaying the fears of the short boy who is afraid he is not growing enough or the tall girl who thinks she will be a giant."

Psychological support from doctor and parents to allay the stress of both short stature and delayed sexual growth is very important while nature takes its course. Occasionally, when the emotional anguish of the teenager is extreme, a physician may suggest speeding up nature's timetable with male hormones (androgens). As we learned in the previous chapter, androgens produce the rapid growth spurt during puberty, but they also stimulate the epiphyseal closure that ends growth altogether. As Dr. Blizzard points out to boys he treats at his Charlottesville clinic, "Testosterone will quickly add a couple of inches along with sexual characteristics, but at a possible cost of closing the epiphyses prematurely and cutting an inch or more off ultimate growth."

So the treatment must be considered carefully. To avert the danger of stopping bone growth too soon, some researchers in recent years have tried giving androgens in small amounts on a discontinuous schedule, usually on daily hormone dosage for a month and then off a month. Bone maturation is tested frequently, and as soon as the patient's bone age catches up with his chronological age, treatment is stopped. NIH reports on one study of 67 boys who underwent this on-and-off therapy, and growth increased to about three inches a year as long as the epiphyses remained open. According to the report, "In most cases, ultimate height attained was no more than that predicted, however, most of the boys achieved this height earlier, and a few even grew taller than expected." The studies still are not conclusive as to whether this intermittent therapy solves the problem of premature closure or if it can promote growth to a height greater than the person's genetic potential.

The biggest problem with the constitutional growth pattern is its *delayed* aspect, which can cause considerable emotional anguish. We'll take a closer look at the psychological problems in chapter 8.

3. INTRAUTERINE GROWTH RETARDATION

Doctors used to call any baby under 5½ pounds at birth a premature infant, even if it was delivered after a full nine months of intrauterine growth. Now physicians are recognizing that prematurity is a separate problem from small, full-term babies, and that one-third to one-half of all newborn infants weighing less than 5½ pounds are suffering from intrauterine growth retardation. The distinction is of paramount importance in providing appropriate postnatal care.

Intrauterine growth retardation implies that some factor has limited growth, and researchers have found many factors to blame. Some are maternal cigarette smoking, maternal high blood pressure, exposure to high altitudes, genetic or chromosomal damage, fetal infection from viruses such as German measles, chronic maternal malnutrition from an early age, and ingestion of certain drugs by the mother. Some of these factors can also be responsible for an associated congenital malformation. Recent studies at the University of Washington Medical Center reveal that not only large amounts of alcohol consumed by the mother can affect the fetus, but also as little as two ounces of alcohol a day can produce "fetal alcohol syndrome" that causes babies to develop smaller than normal.

The size of a baby is closely linked to the size of the placenta, and a frequent cause of low birth weight is a small placenta. Fetal growth is dependent on nutrients and oxygen supplied through the placenta. In some cases part of the placenta pulls away from the uterine wall and the fetus is inadequately nourished. In the next chapter, I'll tell you about Doug, the 11-year-old I mentioned at the beginning of this chapter. He is termed an "intrauterine growth-retarded dwarf," caused by an infarcted placenta. Doug was a full-term baby who measured 3 pounds, 4 ounces in weight and 16 inches in length.

I went to a very interesting talk called "Meanwhile Back at the Womb—Growth Retardation" given by an expert in the pathology of the fetus, Dr. Eugene Perrin, who stated

A three-year-old boy with intrauterine growth retardation and a normal three-year-old girl. (Photo courtesy of Human Growth Foundation)

that most four and a half to five pound full term babies who have no other congenital problems seem to catch up to normal birth weight and proceed to grow similarly to babies of average birth weight. This catch-up growth may occur quickly or it may take as long as three to seven years. But full-term babies under four and a half pounds have little chance for normal growth and a large percentage remain below the third percentile. Their small size may be due to small cells or fewer cells or both. Many scientists suspect that during certain critical periods of growth, both during and after pregnancy, damage to the full potential of growth may be irreversible.

These small babies grow slowly but at a normal maturation rate, so they develop into miniature adults, normal in every way except size. Growth researchers are learning that in some cases which have an associated delay in bone development, human growth hormone therapy is beneficial, as we'll see in the next chapter.

4. BONE DISEASES

According to the Human Growth Foundation, there are more than 100 distinct bone diseases that can affect height from a mild stunting to severe dwarfism. Their medical names are usually tongue-twisters like achondroplasia, hypophosphatasia, mucopolysaccharidoses, osteogenesis imperfecta, and so on. Most of the diseases fall into a group called chondrodystrophies, which means abnormalities of the cartilage portion of the bones.

One of the most common of these is achondroplasia, which is characterized by a disproportionate shortness of the arms and legs while the head is frequently large and the trunk normal size.

Bone X-rays usually reveal the abnormality and permit diagnosis of the underlying disorder. Some forms are inherited and some are not. We'll take a closer look at these disorders and the problems associated with them in later chapters.

5. THYROID HORMONE DEFICIENCY

A deficiency of thyroid hormone is known as hypothyroidism, which may cause slow growth and sometimes mental sluggishness. Babies whose thyroid tissue doesn't develop at all before birth are born with the condition called cretinism and are severely retarded. If thyroid therapy is started immediately at birth, cretins have a good chance of average physical growth, but usually don't attain normal mental capacity.

There are varying degrees of thyroid deficiency and thus varying degrees of retarded growth, both mental and physical. The deficiency may be due to lack of the thyroid-stimulating hormone from the pituitary gland or the inability of the thyroid gland to supply enough of its hormones. When the problem begins any time after birth, proper hormone treatment will usually cause catch-up growth and then a continuing pattern of growth at a normal rate, so the child recovers both mentally and physically as long as therapy continues.

Evidently this cause of short stature can be easily missed when mental problems are not involved. Dr. William H. Daughaday, who is coordinator of endocrinology and metabolism at Washington University School of Medicine in St. Louis, has emphasized that this particular endocrine problem is often overlooked in general practice. He has said, "We see quite a few patients with unrecognized hypothyroidism coming from reasonably good doctors. I think many practicing physicians equate juvenile hypothyroidism with cretinism. They miss the late-onset hypothyroids, who may be perfectly normal in intelligence and apparently quite active."

I remember way back when I was in 8th or 9th grade I had the old "basal metabolism" test for thyroid function. As I remember, I had to go to a lab early in the morning without eating, breathe into a machine, rest, breathe—a very lengthy, unpleasant process that's now a hazy memory of a hard cot, a cold machine, and being hungry. Nowadays, thyroid-hormone deficiency is easy to diagnose with just blood tests. No, nothing was wrong with my thyroid.

6. HYPOPITUITARISM

When growth hormone is absent, in deficient supply, or for some reason does not perform normally, linear growth is stunted by a condition called hypopituitarism. The most common cause is failure of the pituitary gland to produce HGH.

Although usually of normal size at birth (an indication that HGH is not a primary controller of fetal growth), hypopituitary children grow very slowly, usually less than an inch and a half per year. Their extremely short stature, which falls below the three percentile curve, is accompanied by delayed bone growth and often delayed dental age. If left untreated, a perfectly proportioned but short adult is the result. The lack of HGH does not affect intelligence levels at all.

Varying degrees of diminished secretion affect growth differently, so that it's possible for a person with HGH deficiency to grow as tall as 5 feet or perhaps as small as the captivating circus star Michu, who is 33" tall, weighs 25 pounds, and is appearing with Ringling Bros. and Barnum & Bailey Circus billed as "The Smallest Man in the World."

In 1954 when the first International Growth Hormone Symposium was held, the existence of a growth-promoting substance was still in question. By 1978, many thousands of hypopituitary children have been helped to grow to 5 feet or more with injections of growth hormone obtained from human pituitary glands after death. This medical success story is a fascinating one, discussed in the following chapter.

7. NUTRITIONAL SHORT STATURE

Chronic malnutrition will prevent children from reaching their full growth potential. Most common among these are children with protein deficiency. We'll look at how nutrition affects stature in chapter 5.

8. CHROMOSOMAL DISORDERS

Scientists have discovered that a missing or malformed chromosome in body cells may be associated with short stat-

Michu, a popular performer with Ringling Bros. and Barnum & Bailey Circus, is 33 inches short. (Photo courtesy of Ringling Bros. and Barnum & Bailey Circus)

ure. The most common example is called Turner's Syndrome and is found only in girls. They rarely grow to 5 feet tall and have underdeveloped ovaries. A diagnosis is made through analysis of the cell's chromosomes to discover a defect in the sex ("X") chromosomes. (More on that subject later, in the chapter on genetics.) According to Dr. Blizzard, "The physician should think of this possibility in an extremely short girl when there is no other apparent cause. When properly treated, these girls can develop normal sexual characteristics, can menstruate, and can have normal sexual relations. They are unable to conceive and, therefore, adopt children."

9. SECONDARY GROWTH FAILURE

Almost any serious disease can stunt a child's height because growth is so intricately dependent on good health. Slow growth or an irregular growth pattern may be associated with chronic diseases such as kidney, heart, or intestinal disorders. For example, if a digestive problem prevents the absorption of nutrients, one result will be retarded growth. Children who aren't growing due to chronic disease are grouped by physicians in a "failure to thrive" category.

Some diseases, such as severe asthma, kidney disease or arthritis, are treated with large doses of cortisone, and this drug suppresses growth hormone action on bones and tissues. Therefore, growth retardation may result as a side effect to this therapy.

10. PSYCHOSOCIAL SHORT STATURE

This cause of short stature, first called emotional deprivation, was studied and described in a series of 13 patients by Dr. Blizzard when he was at Johns Hopkins in the early 1960's. He found that when emotionally battered children with stunted growth are removed from the suspect home environment, height shoots up promptly in a catch-up spurt. Dr. Blizzard believes this problem is a far more frequent cause of growth failure than has been thought—or can be proved. We'll look at the environmental effects on growth in chapter 5.

THE IMPORTANCE OF BEING AWARE

Yes, I think all parents should be concerned about their child's height. From the time of conception until the epiphyses close, there are dozens of roadblocks that can slow down growth and prevent your child from reaching his tallest potential. So why take a chance? It's so easy to be aware of your child's growth, using the guidelines in this chapter.

If problems develop, the earlier the diagnosis the more chance there might be to correct them. If he can't be helped to grow taller, at least your awareness and support can help your child deal with the psychological problems. I think one of the unkindest reactions a parent can give a short child is, "Don't worry, you'll grow." Nine times out of ten that will be true, but no short kid wants to hear that exact statement from you any more than he wants to hear it from a doctor. It's a brushoff. You will show more understanding and concern if you trade that trite remark in for something like, "It's tough to be small in a tall world, isn't it?"

You know, six feet in length isn't much. Mark it out on the floor and look at it. But when you turn the tape measure up and mark the wall at six feet, that represents a very tall man. Now do the same with five feet, four feet and three feet. A foot isn't much lying there on the floor. But—WOW—what a huge difference it makes in a person's height. Every inch—or centimeter, if you prefer—counts. Do you know how much your child has grown this year?

4 Human Growth Hormone

> *Every pituitary not saved is an extravagant waste.*
> National Pituitary Agency

Susie appeared normal at birth, measuring 20½ inches and weighing 8 pounds 9 ounces. By the time she was a year old she had gained about 6 pounds and grown 7 inches, which is only a little below normal. By age two her growth had slowed down, and between ages 2 and 5 she grew only about 4 inches and was almost a foot shorter than average 5-year-olds. Her problem was diagnosed as hypopituitarism, which is a failure of the pituitary gland to produce adequate growth hormone.

At age 5 Susie's IQ tested between 70 and 80, but the low score was attributed to emotional problems rather than mental retardation. Like many children with growth-hormone deficiency, Susie was shy and had trouble coping with the social stigma of being short.

Human growth hormone (HGH) became available for Susie when she was 6 years old and her height age was less than 2 and her bone age 3. On dosage of 6 mgs. per week she grew 3 inches in 6 months. After 18 months of HGH treatment Susie had gained 8¾ inches. With continued treatment, her height age and bone age are expected to catch up to her chronological age.

Susie is an example of what is medically called hypopituitary dwarfism, which is the cause of about one out of ten cases of abnormally short stature. Her case points out several typical features of HGH deficiency:

1. Her birth size was normal, indicating that some other factor besides HGH controls growth before birth. (Research shows that placental factors and insulin are important to prenatal growth.)
2. Her growth failure began slowly during her first year and increased rapidly after that.
3. Her emotional problems became as great as her physical problems.
4. Bone age dropped at least 2 years lower than chronological age.
5. HGH treatment produced an immediate growth spurt and then a tapering off, but continued to stimulate enough increased growth for eventual attainment of acceptable height.

Susie was fortunate to be diagnosed early in childhood so that the missing growth hormone could be replaced before her bones started to fuse. The earlier in life HGH therapy is begun, the longer time the child has to grow. Once the sex hormones promote epiphyseal closure, further linear growth is impossible.

A hypopituitary dwarf rarely grows more than an inch and a half a year after age three. Slow linear growth accompanied by delayed bone growth are typical symptoms. In the first few months of HGH therapy, typically the child will grow 2 to 3 inches and often increase stature by 3 to 5 inches during the first year. However, continued injections of HGH seem to have a waning effect, and many studies are being done to understand the reasons and to figure out how to sustain the effect of HGH.

Although the overall response to HGH therapy by growth hormone deficient children has been an overwhelming success story with little adverse reaction other than the pain of the shot, some patients do develop antibodies to the administered HGH. Continued improvements in the purification of extracted growth hormone are reducing the incidence of antibody formation, but still the risk exists. In a small percentage of cases resistance to the injected hormone causes growth to halt completely.

Let's look at another case. At a meeting of the Human Growth Foundation it was easy to spot the bursting excitement of one couple there. Finally they made the announcement: their 20 year old son Dan had reached the monumental goal of 5 feet. Later I heard Dan's story, which began with average growth until age 7 or 8.

"At first we weren't too aware of anything," his father, Gerald Parent, said, "but eventually we got concerned when Dan's pants size didn't change for two or three years."

After extensive exams by first the pediatrician and then at a Child Development Center at a major hospital, the diagnosis was a brain tumor. At age 10, Dan had brain surgery. As his father explained, "They not only removed the tumor but also the pituitary gland which had been engulfed by the growth."

Without a pituitary gland, Dan's body was missing several important hormones, including HGH, but over the years his hormone therapy has enabled him slowly to grow and mature into a normal adult. As of this writing Dan measures five feet one and one-half inches (his mother, Sheila Parent, told me, "Don't leave out that half inch, it's *very* important!"). Although his remaining growing time is limited because of his age, the therapy is still working.

Dan's case shows one cause of growth hormone deficiency —brain lesions that prevent the pituitary gland from functioning. But in many cases, like Susie's, the cause of the pituitary gland not producing adequate HGH is unknown.

In rare instances the other 3 types of hormones secreted by the anterior lobe of the pituitary (the hormones that give chemical orders to the thyroid gland, adrenal glands and sex glands) are missing too, and without treatment these children do not grow up in either height or sexual development. When all four of these vital pituitary hormones are lacking, the condition has two medical labels: panhypopituitarism or asexual ateliotic dwarfism. These individuals are normally proportioned and have a normal range of intelligence, but since they never develop into mature men and women, their bodies and faces remain childlike. Because the sex hormones that cause maturity are never triggered into production, the cartilage plates at the growing ends of the bones are not closed. Theoretically these little people are still capable of growth even in their 20's and 30's, although HGH therapy is less effective than in children.

Through radioimmunoassay testing techniques developed in the 1960's that measure the tiny amounts of hormones in the blood, scientists have learned that it's possible for the pituitary gland to function normally except for the production of adequate HGH. This isolated deficiency, called hypopituitarism or sexual ateliotic dwarfism, also causes short stature, but these people do develop mature sexual characteristics during their teenage years. Their cartilage plates are gradually replaced by bone at about the normal age, or slightly later.

Without hormone treatment these dwarfs can grow to about four to four and a half feet, although many are much shorter. Even though they don't lack sex hormones, usually adult voices are high-pitched and facial skin is soft and wrinkled, giving them all a similar appearance.

A deficiency of growth hormone prevents growth in height, but apparently has little other effect on the body, although children receiving HGH injections usually fatigue less readily. Neither body proportions, intelligence levels, general health nor life expectancy are affected by lack of HGH. Sexual functions are not impaired, although delivery must be by Caesarean section.

Even though he lived a hundred years ago, Charles S. Stratton is still one of the most famous examples of a hypopituitary dwarf. Promoted by P.T. Barnum as General Tom Thumb, Stratton began his circus career at about age 6 and 25 inches tall. Although over nine pounds at birth, this tiny boy who captured the attention of the world finally reached 3 feet 4 inches. His small size, however, did not diminish his brain power, as many people are apt to believe of anyone who is small, and his performing ability earned him a fortune. Nor was his sexual maturation affected. A photo shows him with a beard, and at age 23 he fell madly in love with Barnum's newest midget attraction, 32-inch-tall Lavinia Bump. Lavinia was also perfectly proportioned. At age 13 she had taught school standing on a desk so her pupils could see her. The couple's wedding was attended by thousands. The newlyweds were received at the White House by President Lincoln, who is said to have made the observation: "God likes to do funny things; here you have the long and the short of it." Rumor tells that the Strattons had a baby daughter, but Barnum occasionally hired babies to pose as offspring of his midgets, so the rumor remains unproven.

Now scientists believe that both Stratton and his wife were victims of isolated growth hormone deficiency, and if in childhood they could have been injected with shots of HGH they would have grown much taller. Now there's a question to ponder—in Tom Thumb's case would bigger have meant better?

Although probably the most famous midget in history, Tom Thumb was by no means the smallest. *Guinness Book of World Records* lists the shortest mature human of whom there is accurate record as Pauline Musters, a Dutch girl who measured 12 inches at birth in 1876. Only 23.2 inches short before she died at age 19, "Princess Pauline" weighed nine pounds at her heaviest.

Just as the lack of sufficient HGH will stunt growth, so the extreme overproduction of HGH will produce too much growth. In childhood, overabundance of HGH causes the long bones to grow in enormous excess, resulting in giantism. Robert Wadlow, the 8-foot-11¾-inch giant mentioned earlier, grew to the tallest height ever scientifically verified. According to the *Book of Lists,* the tallest man now living is Don Koehler, a resident of Chicago, Illinois, who measures 8 feet, 2 inches. The tallest woman, at 7 feet, 7¼ inches, 23-year-old Sandy Allen, underwent surgery last year for the removal of a tumor on her pituitary gland which was causing the excessive supply of HGH, so Sandy has finally stopped growing.

When excessive secretion of HGH begins after the epiphyses close, it doesn't affect the person's height, but there can be a grotesque increase in size of fingers, toes, forehead, jaw and internal organs. This rare condition is called acromegaly.

Overproduction of HGH can now be detected just as readily as its deficiency, so giantism and acromegaly can be diagnosed before body growth is extremely distorted. The treatment for either condition usually involves removal of a tumor and/or of the pituitary gland itself, or its destruction by radiation.

Today, growth specialists estimate that there are about 5,000 to 10,000 children in the U.S. with hypopituitarism. Ever since Dr. Maurice Raben, the "father of growth hormone," first used HGH in children in 1957 and demonstrated that it makes hypopituitary children grow, evidence has overwhelmingly supported his findings. However, there's one big problem, which another set of worried parents ran up against in 1960 when their son Jeff was diagnosed as having hypopituitarism. The father, psychiatrist Alvin Balaban, who became one of the primary founders of the Human Growth Foundation, told of his reaction and subsequent problems at an HGF meeting:

"I remembered that back in medical school, hypopituitarism was a small chapter in a textbook on medicine, about children like Tom Thumb, and that you couldn't do anything about it. I asked, 'Can anything be done for Jeff?' The physician replied, 'Well, they've recently started doing some work with something called human growth hormone, and it seems to be very effective.' I said, 'That's great, give him human growth hormone.' She said, 'Well, it only comes from pituitary glands and they can only come from autopsies.' And I said, 'Well, that's okay, we don't mind.' She laughed and said it was very difficult to come by and whatever the hospital had available was already committed to one or two children. I asked, 'What happens now?' She replied, 'Well, you'd better start searching among your friends and see if you know a pathologist. Maybe you can get some glands. And if you can get together a hundred glands, we can start him on a course of treatment.'"

That's the kicker. HGH must come from human pituitary glands removed during autopsy. Dr. Raben and many other scientists learned that growth hormone from an animal of lower species such as a cow or pig does not work in humans, unlike other hormones such as insulin or thyroxine. Monkey growth hormone works a little, but hardly enough to make it worth the effort of extraction. As mentioned earlier, growth hormone is what scientists call "species specific."

Another thing scientists have learned about HGH is that it's a giant, complex protein molecule that's very difficult to synthesize in the laboratory. It's made up of a chain of 191 amino-acid units. The coiled-chain sequence of amino acids was presented in 1966 by Choh Hao Li of the University of California and was later modified by Hugh Niall of the Massachusetts General Hospital. Dr. Choh achieved synthesis of HGH in the laboratory in 1961, but the manufacture of a biologically active hormone in sufficient quantities for clinical use is still years away. Dr. Choh and other scientists are working on this problem, and one approach that seems headed for some success is synthesizing the fragment of the protein molecule that apparently acts as the power portion. In other words, maybe they don't need to call in the whole orchestra if just the piano will do the job. However, this won't be an immediate answer to the need for HGH, because even when the scientists have synthesized HGH effectively, it will take 3 to 5 years to pass through the FDA's screening program and be permitted for use. Another avenue is being explored at Scripps Clinic and Research Foundation, where biochemists have found an enzyme that triples the biological activity of growth hormone.

So, if your child, like Susie, Dan, and Jeff, needs HGH to grow, there's only one place to get it—from a human pituitary gland of someone who has died. And one gland won't do much good, because usually at least 100 glands are needed to treat one child for one year, and many children need treatment for at least 10 years.

At the time the Balabans needed pituitaries, neither the

National Pituitary Agency, which is in charge of pituitary gland collection, nor the Human Growth Foundation, which helps NPA in many ways, had been formed. But somehow the Balabans had to get HGH for Jeff, so they sent out 400 letters to everybody they could think of, hoping that some of the people knew pathologists who could get them pituitary glands. As Dr. Balaban recounts the story, "Nothing happened for a few days, and suddenly the telephone started ringing, the doorbell started ringing and pituitary glands started arriving in the mail. It was the most incredible kind of experience. We said, 'Where in the world are these coming from?' California, Florida, Canada—from all over the place they started coming in—one, two, five, ten. We were away for Christmas visiting a friend, and we arrived home Christmas evening to find a special delivery package of three different mailings of pituitary glands which brought us to the hundred. And we dashed off a telegram to Jeff's physician saying, 'Merry Christmas, we have a hundred glands.' "

By June of '62 the Balabans had over a thousand pituitary glands stockpiled in their freezer for Jeff, which eventually they turned over to the National Pituitary Agency for distribution to other children who needed HGH treatment, with the stipulation that Jeff could have all the HGH his therapy required.

The National Pituitary Agency was started in 1963, and its chief instigator and first medical director was Dr. Robert Blizzard. In 1965, with the help of the Balabans and other parents of children with growth problems, the Human Growth Foundation was formed with the original purpose of helping the NPA collect pituitary glands. The HGF is strictly a volunteer organization and the NPA is a government-funded arm of the National Institutes of Health and is sponsored by the College of American Pathologists.

The National Pituitary Agency is in charge of collecting the glands from pathologists, extracting the HGH and other hormones, and distributing the HGH to physicians whose research projects qualify for HGH. You cannot, in this country, go out to the drug store and buy HGH for your short child. You can't buy it at all. The supply is so scarce that its use must be controlled so that the neediest children get it and they must be subjects of research programs that will advance the medical world's knowledge about this important hormone.

Pituitary glands are hard to get. Part of the problem is the declining rate of autopsies in this country. With our advanced medical techniques, an autopsy is required less often to establish cause of death. As Terry Cole of the NPA explained to me, until about four years ago, hospitals were required for accreditation to perform a certain percentage of autopsies. When that requirement was dropped, autopsies became a needless hospital expense in many cases. In addition, funeral homes frequently advise against autopsies so their work won't be more difficult. There's no question that a grieving family does not enjoy the image of their loved one being "violated," and undertakers play upon these feelings.

If you die in a hospital, your next-of-kin must sign a consent form for an autopsy, which includes a line for the specified permission of tissue removal. If you die out of a hospital in a sudden death, your body becomes property of the state and the medical examiner or coroner (whichever system your state has) is in charge. Did you know that only six states have laws authorizing the medical examiner or coroner to extract tissue during autopsy? HGF chapters in other states are promoting the passage of laws to facilitate pituitary gland removal by all pathologists. For effective use, the glands should be removed and properly stored within 48 hours after death.

All states recognize the Anatomical Gift Act, which legalizes the "Uniform Donor Card." (see Figure 13) Many states are distributing these cards with driver's licenses, and some (e.g. Arizona) even print the information on the back of the license. Through this card you can indicate your willingness to donate your kidneys, eyes, or other parts of the body needed for transplanting, or your pituitary gland, which can't be transplanted, but which is at this time our only source of HGH.

88   Growing Up Small

UNIFORM DONOR CARD

OF _____
Print or type name of donor

In the hope that I may help others, I hereby make this anatomical gift, if medically acceptable, to take effect upon my death. The words and marks below indicate my desires:

I give: (a) _____ any needed organs or parts

(b) _____ only the following organs or parts

_____
Specify the organ(s) or part(s)

for the purposes of transplantation, therapy, medical research or education;

(c) _____ my body for anatomical study if needed.

Limitations or special wishes, if any: _____

Signed by the donor and the following two witnesses in the presence of each other:

_____   _____
Signature of Donor   Date of Birth of Donor

_____   _____
Date Signed   City & State

_____   _____
Witness   Witness

This is a legal document under the Uniform Anatomical Gift Act or similar laws.

For further information consult your physician.

Fig. 13. Both sides of a Uniform Donor Card

Of course NPA and HGF promote the campaign, along with the Kidney Foundation and other groups, to get all of us to sign the donor cards and carry them with us. When signed and witnessed properly, the donor card constitutes a legal will and technically a physician can remove body parts without permission from the next of kin, but few doctors would do so. So it's wise for you to inform your next of kin of your wishes.

For a short child to benefit from your supply of HGH, you and your next of kin first must be willing to donate your pituitary gland, and an autopsy of your body including your head must be performed. I mention the latter only to clue you in on the fact that along with the declining autopsy rate, only a third of the post mortems include a cranial exam.

Terry Cole is one of NPA's three messengers who travel all over the country picking up frozen glands. Many thousands of the glands are preserved and mailed directly to the NPA by the so-called "acetone" method that Dr. Raben perfected. But many more thousands are now frozen because recent improvements in extraction methods are securing a purer hormone in almost triple the amount from a frozen gland compared to an acetone gland.

NPA's pituitary-gland collection rose from 11,057 in 1963 to a peak of 83,107 in 1975. The 1977 total dipped down to 64,867, a decrease that reflects the discontinued use of embalmed pituitaries because of the comparatively small yield. Of the 64,867 glands collected, a little less than half were frozen. The average yield from an acetone-preserved gland is about 4–5 mg., but a frozen gland yields 10–12 mg. of HGH. So, although the total number of glands collected is decreasing, the amount of usable HGH is increasing.

But the frozen glands can't be mailed. As Terry Cole explains, "Pituitaries are harvested and maintained in dry ice and kept deep frozen at all times. They are collected on a regularly scheduled basis every four to six months . . . returned to the National Pituitary Agency, batched in large lots and transported to the west coast for extraction."

By the way, all the NPA pays the hospitals for the glands is a $2.00 reimbursement fee to cover storage costs. It is against the law to buy or sell human tissue.

Dr. Salvatore Raiti, director of NPA, picks up the story: "The pituitary glands are homogenized. Using several chemical steps, the product is separated into two factions: (a) glycoprotein, (b) growth hormone and other residues. Later the glycoproteins are separated into FSH, LH and TSH (the gonad- and thyroid-stimulating hormones). The growth hormone is further purified . . . prepared in vials suitable for human use . . . all tests to insure its sterility and purity are carried out. The NPA distributes the hormone to qualified investigators for research purposes throughout the USA."

Since NPA's program began in 1963, about 3,000 hypopituitary children have been helped to grow taller. For several years the lists of youngsters waiting in line for treatment were very long and there was only enough HGH available to help a small percentage of those who needed it. Now the bulk of children diagnosed as hypopituitary are receiving proper therapy. Dr. Raiti estimates that about 1,000 youngsters are currently receiving the hormone.

Until 1977 the cutoff point for continued therapy was 5 feet in order to provide HGH to as many patients as possible. Improved extraction methods now allow the NPA to permit treatment to a new cutoff level of 5 feet 4 inches. But, as Dr. Raiti explains, "These children grow more under the influence of sex hormones. So they may reach 5'6" to 5'8", which is reasonable."

Although the current supply seems to be keeping up with the demand as far as hypopituitary children are concerned, the declining autopsy rate is a constant threat to the source of supply. In addition, far more HGH is needed for research. Other types of short stature may respond to large doses, but so far not enough hormone has been available for the necessary experimentation. The NPA claims that "the number of glands needed for therapy and research is approximately 75% of the deaths per year in the U.S." The current annual death rate is close to two million.

How do you feel about donating your pituitary gland after death? Perhaps you hesitate to sign a donor card because of religious reasons, but most religions encourage the donation of vital body parts. Or perhaps your reaction is like my 5-foot-7-inch brother's: "Why would anyone want my pituitary gland? I stopped growing a long time ago!"

When extraction of HGH from human pituitaries was first started, it became rapidly evident that almost all pituitaries, young and old alike, yield approximately the same amount of hormone. Dr. Raiti explains: "The content of the pituitary gland is similar in all pituitaries on a basis of weight . . . naturally smaller glands have less total hormone. Only a small amount (about 1%–2%) is secreted each day into the bloodstream. The rest is stored in the pituitary and we do not know why large stores are needed. Adult pituitaries as well as those of children store the hormone. It is needed not only for growth but also for carbohydrate, fat and protein metabolism."

Evidence is accumulating that HGH is an overall regulator of many metabolic processes in the body. The supply of this important hormone is replenished throughout life, although scientists don't know why. Hypopituitary people who no longer receive injections after the 5'4" cutoff point are not usually adversely affected by the lack of growth hormone, nor does the lack seem to bother the health of hypopituitary dwarfs who have never received HGH therapy.

Many of the avenues of HGH research over the last 20 years I find very tantalizing. Here are some selected items reported through the National Pituitary Agency and/or the Human Growth Foundation:

Item #1:

The release of HGH into the bloodstream is promptly and massively stimulated by a fall of blood sugar levels. Its relationship to blood sugar establishes it as an important cog in the body's energy metabolism machinery, and many studies concentrate on the interwoven mysteries of HGH, insulin, hypoglycemia and diabetes.

Item #2:

HGH is not released from the pituitary at a steady rate. Instead, it stops and goes sporadically, under the control of many different influences. Scientists have learned that two important body activities that stimulate HGH secretion into the bloodstream are deep sleep (regardless of the time of night or day) and exercise.

However, don't jump to the conclusion that if your child sleeps 15 hours instead of 8 or exercises 10 hours instead of 3 that he'll grow more—it doesn't work that way. In the first place, the normal daily concentration of HGH is 4–5 mg./ml. in children (1 mg. = .000035 of one ounce), and a normally functioning body probably won't produce a substantial amount of extra HGH no matter what you do to it. In addition, growth is produced by the reaction of your cells to the hormone, and most short-statured persons have the same amount of HGH supply as tall people. However, when the body does not function normally and it's exposed to extreme deprivations, then HGH secretion is frequently affected.

The stimulation of HGH secretion by exercise is being used

in a testing procedure. As explained by Dr. Robert Blizzard in his summary of NPA's 1973 symposium on "Advances in HGH Research": "Following a 4 hour fast, exercise for 20 minutes is carried out and blood drawn. A second specimen is drawn 20 minutes later. 80% of normals will have significant GH at that time."

Item #3:

The "master gland," the pituitary, has a master of its own —the hypothalamus, which is the area of the brain to which the pituitary is joined (see diagram in chapter 2), and they are in communication through connecting blood vessels. Dr. Roger Guillemin of the Salk Institute in California has discovered a powerful hypothalamic factor, called somatostatin, which stops HGH secretion, thereby controlling the pituitary's output of HGH in the blood.

Scientists have found a hypothalamic GH-releasing factor in some animals, which has the opposite affect of somatostatin, but so far such control has not been pinpointed in our species. Pediatric endocrinologist David Mosier, Jr. of the University of California, who is one of the many doctors researching the controls of physical growth, comments, "I don't believe that identification and synthesis of a specific growth hormone-releasing factor is in the cards for the near future. A number of substances are now competing for the honor." In the meantime, research continues on the inhibiting influence of somatostatin.

Item #4:

One of the hottest areas of current HGH research involves a substance called somatomedin. It has been learned that HGH promotes growth not by acting directly on growing tissue but by controlling somatomedin, which exerts several biologic effects on cartilage. At the basic molecular level, it is somatomedin that enables the cartilage cells to incorporate the chemicals and nutrients they need to produce growing bone. So far, no organ has been found richer in somatomedin than blood plasma, but there is evidence that the liver is the major generation site. It's not clear yet whether HGH stimulates the liver to make somatomedin anew, or if it's made from a part of the much larger HGH molecule.

The intertwining relationships between height, HGH and somatomedin (SM) are confusing. The report from the 1973 NPA symposium on HGH research states that in certain patients with normal growth, HGH was absent but SM levels were normal. Conversely, certain dwarfs have been diagnosed to have normal HGH secretion but are low in somatomedin. On the other hand, the report says, "Normal, short and tall children showed no correlations between height and SM levels."

Among other scientists, Dr. Judson J. VanWyk, who heads the pediatric endocrinology clinic at the University of North Carolina Hospital, is trying to purify enough of this substance to determine its chemical structure and to eventually synthesize it, which isn't a remote possibility as it's already known that it's only one-third to one-fifth the molecular size of HGH. However, extracting enough of the stuff to study it is very difficult because it exists in the blood in very tiny amounts. Dr. VanWyk and his colleagues have, in fact, extracted only milligram quantities from a *ton* of human plasma. Dr. VanWyk says that laboratory studies of the purified simple protein substance show "it's certainly potent enough to hold promise of a growth-promoting pharmacologic role sometime in the future."

Somatomedin research may open up some exiting possibilities for understanding other growth problems besides growth hormone deficiency, such as Turner's syndrome and achondroplasia.

Item #5:

HGH is believed to be useful in therapies other than linear growth. Because it affects carbohydrate, fat and protein metabolism, it may prove useful in hastening the healing of burns and fractures. Because it raises blood sugar levels, it may be helpful in treating hypoglycemia. It could perhaps be used in obesity because it mobilizes fat and utilizes fatty acids for caloric needs. Other research projects are investigating the possible use of HGH in treating diseases such as muscular dystrophy or osteoporosis, and the effects of HGH on blood-cholesterol levels.

Item #6:

In Europe autopsies are the rule rather than the exception, and a Swedish pharmaceutical company, Kabi, processes enough HGH to meet most of the need in European countries and Japan. The Kabi GH is being investigated for use in this country, and FDA approval is also being sought for selling imported HGH by an American company, Calbiochem. Dr. Raiti points out that the Kabi and Calbiochem products are expensive—about $7.50 per one International Unit (an IU approximates 1 mg). He explains, "The average child needs a minimum of 6 IU per week or about $2,500 per year or more." That's a far cry from the less than $1.50 per IU of our tax money that pays for HGH to be supplied free by the NPA to researchers and their patients.

Item #7:

Can HGH injections help genetically short children grow taller? Well, the correct answer to that question is that the proof isn't in. There simply isn't enough HGH available to do the necessary experimenting. So far, top priority goes to kids with proven HGH deficiency because they will benefit most from the therapy.

Most of the scientists I've contacted tell me that additional HGH probably won't help any child with normal HGH supply to grow taller. Dr. Raiti says, "Familial short stature probably cannot be helped. These children secrete all the hormone they need and a lot more is stored in their pituitary. However, large quantities have *not* been administered to them for a long time (there isn't enough hormone to do this). The risks, if any, of such treatment would also have to be evaluated."

Scientists think that injections of HGH effectively promote growth only when bone age lags behind chronological age. Usually genetically short people just grow a little less, but at a steady rate, with bone age keeping in step with chronological birthdays.

Evidently too much HGH might not be a good thing, even in

a short person. Dr. Mosier explained to me that: "In order to overcome short stature in an individual with normal endocrine function one would have to produce an abnormal situation which might lead to the development of the same complications one sees in pituitary giantism due to excess production of growth hormone. These complications include diabetes mellitus, bone and joint disorders, and other problems."

Both Dr. Hoffman and Dr. Raiti added a note of doom to the idea by telling me that it is probable the addition of HGH causes the body's own HGH production to shut down, at least temporarily, and perhaps permanently.

However, as I said before, the proof is not all in. Many studies have been done with HGH injections in non-hypopituitary dwarfs, and sometimes added growth was a benefit without negative side effects. Several such cases were reported at the 1973 NPA symposium. Here is a statement that I particularly applaud from a team of researchers headed by Dr. John Crawford of Massachusetts General:

> With our presently limited supplies, we have been able to provide practical help only to those lacking GH. Yet nature's experiment of pituitary giantism and the frequency with which some acceleration of growth is seen in patients with constitutional short stature, gonadal dysgenesis [Turner's syndrome] or dwarfism associated with low birth weight tempts the speculation that with the advent of unlimited supplies of this hormone [HGH], somatomedin or the hypothalamic releasing factor, clinicians may be in a position to bring relief to many more short children than can be helped today.

To help more short children grow taller we need more research, which, of course, takes money. Funding growth-research is not a number-one government priority, but the National Institutes of Health does support many research centers in medical institutions across the country. The Human Growth Foundation raises funds for growth research. There were 77 grant proposals totaling a need for $441,000 submitted to HGF's 1977 Research Grants Program. HGF could fund only 5 of the requests, totaling $27,950. Obviously, the need is great.

In addition to raising money for growth research, the Human Growth Foundation continues to aid the National Pituitary Agency in collection of pituitary glands and registration of organ donors. In working toward their goal of eliminating growth disorders, HGF has a program of wide public education to provide information on growth to both physicians and the community. But perhaps HGF's most vital service is creating a meeting ground for short-statured children and their parents. Through a network of 21 chapters across the country, families can share experiences, discuss mutual problems, and find moral support and medical aid.

HGF is really just a group of parents, a group of wonderful, caring, loving parents who got involved because they were worried about their children's growth. They care enough to devote their time and energy to a cause that helps not only their own children, but all children.

My experience with HGF has been heartwarming and inspiring, and one of the many rewards has been getting to know Barbara Taylor and her son Douglas. Using his story to wind up this chapter on growth hormone seems appropriate as Doug's little bottom gets a shot of HGH every other night. Barbara and I had a long chat one day, while her three-year-old played noisily beside us, her Great Dane barked and her phone rang. Aside from serving as current president of the local HGF chapter, Barbara also devotes time to the American Cancer Society, works as an interior designer and is a homemaker, wife, and mother of Margaret, 13, Sam, 3, and Doug, who is 11. So she's busy to say the least, and the atmosphere was hectic but very homey. I came away from that chat not feeling sorry for Doug because he's so short, but feeling that he's a very lucky boy to be raised with such tender, loving, intelligent care. Barbara has some very definite ideas and philosophies on how to treat a short child and how to handle her own feelings as his mother, which I'll go into in chapter

8 when we discuss "Non-Growing Pains." For now, here's the story of Doug's "painfully slow" growth as his mother relates it.

He was a full-term baby, born December 7, 1966, round and normal looking—except he was very small, weighing 3 pounds, 4 ounces and measuring 16 inches. The placenta had partly pulled away from the uterine wall during pregnancy and was badly infarcted and scarred. It was apparent that Doug's small birth size was caused by a nutritional deficiency because part of the placenta had not functioned, probably since about the 5th month of pregnancy as Barbara had some slight bleeding at that time. She had not been ill during her pregnancy, didn't smoke or drink, and didn't take any drugs except vitamins. The tiny baby contracted a staph infection in the hospital and by 10 days of age had dropped to a pound and a half. He wasn't expected to live. But Doug was strong and full-term in gestational age, although termed a "preemie" because of his size. After the infection cured, the hospital wouldn't release him until he weighed 5 pounds. That took two months. At this time the main concern was the question of brain damage and mental retardation. But evidently Doug's brain was never deprived, as Barb modestly says with a happy smile, "By some miracle he's a gifted child with an IQ of 145."

Doug was a healthy baby after his bout with staph, but he grew slowly. At 15 months he was 27 inches and 16 pounds, and by two years he'd only increased to 29½ inches and 19 pounds. Average two-year-olds are about 35 inches. Barb credits her pediatrician for being very alert to Doug's growth problems (unlike many doctors, she adds), and when Doug was two the doctor encouraged Barb to take him to a hospital for special testing. At that time they were living in Minnesota, and Dr. Henry Sauls, who is now chairman of HGF's Medical Advisory Committee, was with the growth research center at the University of Minnesota.

Can you imagine leaving your two-year-old child at a hospital for a week for extensive testing, some of it uncomfortable and all of it certainly unpleasant for a baby? Barb had the courage to do it, although in retrospect she feels that if they had let her stay at the hospital it would have been easier. The coming and going every day was difficult for both her and Doug. The testing showed a normal HGH response. Dr. Sauls's diagnosis: "Intrauterine growth retardation with secondary growth failure." He explained that the cells didn't divide as rapidly as they should have during fetal development, but that Doug was "perfectly proportioned and absolutely all there," as Barb describes him. Dr. Sauls said Doug's growth hormone production was normal for him, and that he would continue to grow, but slowly. He predicted adult height to be about 4'8" to 4'10".

I asked Barbara how she felt about that diagnosis. She said, "I felt terribly guilty . . . I wished I could wave a magic wand and make the child grow." She feels that the advice Dr. Sauls gave her and her husband on how to treat Doug was very valuable . . . "You need to be reminded over and over every day, every week, not to treat a child by his looks but by his chronological age."

The Taylors continued to have physicians follow Doug's growth pattern, and they joined the Human Growth Foundation. By the time Doug was 7, they knew that if there was any help anywhere it would be through HGH research, although up to that time HGH treatment was reserved for hypopituitary children, and Doug didn't qualify.

In his 8th year Doug went to Dr. Robert Thompson at the University of Iowa for routine measuring and bone-age testing. A few months after that came the momentous phone call from Iowa to the Taylors' home in Michigan: Dr. Jerome Grunt at the University of Missouri was conducting a special study of intrauterine growth-retarded children and their response to HGH therapy, and Dr. Thompson thought Doug would qualify.

He did. In fact, he was perfectly suited for the research program because his growth had been carefully documented since birth and because he was still in that vital 6 to 10 age range when children seem to respond best to HGH injections.

In Kansas City, Dr. Grunt explained to the Taylors that thus far his study indicated that 40% of children with Doug's problem had increased growth with HGH therapy, and in rare cases the foreign HGH produced allergies that prevented all further growth. So, there was a 60% chance the shots, which would be painful, wouldn't work at all, and about a .03% chance they would stop Doug's growth altogether. And to get the program started Doug would have to spend 2½ weeks in the Kansas City hospital for testing as part of the research project. So the Taylors were presented with hope, but it was hardly on a silver platter.

Doug's HGH treatment began in May of 1976 when he was 9½. In two years he grew 6 whole inches, to a height of about 4 feet. Yes, Doug is one of the fortunate 40% group.

Doug hasn't had any side effects except the pain of the shot. He's very healthy, his appetite is enormous (he tops the scales at a rousing 45 pounds), and he's very active and athletic (his favorite sport is basketball, both as participant and spectator).

When HGH treatment was started his bone age lagged behind his chronological age by about 18 months and has remained that way. Since at age 11 he's about the size of a 7 year old, Barb wishes his bone age were a good 4 years behind, as that would mean more potential growth. His increased rate of about 2½ inches per year with the additional HGH has been steady. When hypopituitary children are given HGH, they usually respond with an initial quick catch-up growth period that helps them attain normal height. But since Doug hasn't been deficient in the hormone his growth rate remains steady. Barb says, "Douggie's doctor makes no promises . . . hopefully he'll reach 5 feet tall." His final height will depend largely on when and how his body reacts to the adolescent growth spurt. But the outlook seems bright for Doug to reach at least that giant mark of 5 feet, which is miles above the original projection of 4'8" to 4'10". I ought to know—I'm 4'9", remember?

Doug's medical history is a testimonial to the great strides in HGH research. But perhaps it's even more important as a testament to parents wishing they could "wave a magic wand to make a child grow."

Human growth hormone isn't a magic wand, but it is one little sprinkle of stardust that helps a lot of kids, and maybe it would help a lot more if we could just increase the supply. There are two ways you can help, and you can accomplish one or both by calling your nearest Human Growth Foundation chapter. Just say: "Hi. I'd like to make sure a child will get my growth hormone after I don't need it any more." Then, if possible, please add: "I'd also like to make a donation toward growth research."

I'm not sure if HGH could have helped me to grow taller. I stopped growing when I was about 14, which was in 1951—long before clinical use of HGH was possible. Many doctors I've consulted in research for this book have told me HGH can't help genetically short people, and there's no doubt I was born into a short family. As further proof of my "normal" endocrine system they look at my properly proportioned, obviously mature, busty body and say something akin to "there's nothing wrong with you—you are what you're meant to be. Love it!" Well, I do, but how about 5 feet instead of 4'9"? Wow, that's a whole 3 inches and I'd still be short! And those 3 inches would help me drive a car, reach the dinner glasses, and maybe stop little boys from pointing and giggling at me. I'm *so* much shorter than the rest of my short family that I can't help but wonder if my pituitary was just a little lazy. If I could have made it to 5 feet, a girl in school named Fluffy Friestedt promised me she'd throw a big party to honor the event. Okay, I didn't make it. But maybe there's another tiny redhead out there who can, if only we can supply our scientists with enough HGH to do the necessary research.

The significance of such research is reflected in letters written by children or parents thanking pathologists for their help in supplying human growth hormone. Here are excerpts from a few, made available by the Human Growth Foundation, Inc.:

> I am writing to you as the mother of a child who because of an underfunctioning pituitary gland, would

have been destined to the life of a midget had she not been fortunate enough to receive human growth hormone as part of a research investigation. We waited six long years before our daughter Gwenny could receive human growth hormone. Her rate of growth previously was approximately one half inch per year—and now after having been on human growth hormone for eighteen months, she has grown five inches. Gwenny is twelve years old and is 47 inches tall.
Its difficult to put into words the joyful feeling that we have knowing that Gwenny now has possibilities of reaching a reasonable adult height.

Fall brings a new exciting school year for young people of all ages, shapes and sizes. Unfortunately, there are many who are smaller—alot smaller—than their classmates. This leaves them open to ridicule and out of many activities. Our son, Chris, was one of these "little" people. Ten years ago when he was 9 years old, he was only 38 inches tall. Now, thanks to you and others like you he has grown to a near normal height of 5 ft. We know he could never have had this opportunity without growth hormone therapy.

In our area there has been a decrease in the number of autopsies this year so we want to encourage all of you who contribute glands to the National Pituitary Agency to keep up the good work and help make growth possible for many more children who need this treatment so desperately.

Five weeks ago I started receiving H.G.H. which is made available by your cooperation with the National Pituitary Agency. Without your help I would never be taller than 4' 3". Now I am growing again!

Our son, Brian, has been a recipient of growth hormone for the past year and has grown four inches. It has been a miraculous experience for us made possible by you and other considerate pathologists.

The complexities of growth are taken for granted by so many, but I have experienced growth through the sacrifices and dedication of others. I wish to thank you, and those who work with you, for making it possible for me to reach a reasonable adult height. Without growth hormone therapy, I barely grow an inch per year.

For the first time in many years, I do not dread the fall with the 'back to school' movement. For the first time my daughter will not have to defend the right to be in the class her promotion card indicates. She has now attained an acceptable height for her peers.

5 Effects of Eating and Loving

*Better is a dinner of herbs where love is,
than a fatted ox and hatred therewith.*
Proverbs 15.17

"How do you expect to grow if you don't eat?" Sound familiar? Or how about this phrase at a birthday party: "And here's one [WHACK] to grow on!" or, "Here's a pinch [OUCH] to grow an inch!"

These are common testimonies to the importance of food and love in the process of growth. (Well, spanking and pinching at birthday time are supposed to be signs of affection, aren't they?) Environmental influences from birth through puberty provide a large part of the final answer to "how tall are you?" Nutrition, illness, socioeconomic level, emotion, sleep, exercise and other factors can affect growth rates just as crucially as biological factors such as sex, maturation rate, body build and genetic influences. Many of these environmental aspects we've touched on earlier, but in this chapter let's zero in on two items that parents can control to a large extent: eating and loving.

Protein and Calories

A body grows larger by two means: an increase in the number of cells and an increase in the size of cells. According to National Institutes of Health reports, nutritionists are learning that caloric intake influences the rate of cell multiplication, whereas cell size is more dependent on protein consumption. These two—proteins and calories—are the two basic necessities for normal growth.

Have you seen the photos taken in African countries or other developing nations of starving children with swollen stomachs? They are victims of kwashiorkor, a disease caused by chronic lack of protein. In addition to swelling of the abdomen with water, vulnerability to illness, and marked apathy, these children also suffer severe growth retardation. Many of them tested have remarkably small cells for their ages. They are not necessarily starving for a quantity of food but rather for the quality of protein.

Extreme emaciation also occurs frequently in developing nations due to insufficient calories. A calorie, as we all learned in school, measures the energy produced by food when oxidized in the body. Growth, like all functions of the body, is work and needs fuel to operate. Usually the body's energy needs are supplied by the converting of carbohydrates and fats, but protein can be burned for energy also. If the fuel supply from fresh or stored carbohydrates and fats isn't sufficient, the demanding cells grab the protein. In severe cases the body actually devours itself by consuming structural protein. This extreme deprivation of calories during the childhood growth years results in the disease called marasmus, which is characterized by growth retardation and emaciation of body tissues due to starvation.

According to the NIH, in developing nations an estimated 300 million children suffer from marasmus, kwashiorkor, or a combination of both. Recent improvements in nutrition therapies have shown that renewed growth for these children best occurs with a high-calorie diet that is only minimally adequate in protein and heavily concentrated with carbohydrates. When starving children are put on a high-protein diet, studies show that after the first few days their bodies react as though they were not being fed enough calories. The protein is used for energy rather than growth, and growth remains retarded. It is essential that children's diets consist of all three food components—protein, carbohydrate and fat—to promote normal growth so that the cells can both enlarge and multiply.

If you think that children are starving only in remote corners of the world, you'll be surprised to hear that recent HEW studies of the lowest economic level of the U.S. population reveal marked protein and calorie deficiency. Poverty areas on Indian reservations, in Appalachia, in the Southeast, and in large-city ghettos are particularly affected, and many children in these areas are victims of kwashiorkor or marasmus. According to one government report, "Studies show that the average height of poorly nourished American children in the 1-to-6 age group is from 5 to 15 percent lower than that of their well nourished contemporaries."

On the other hand, as we noticed in an earlier chapter, improved nutrition in many areas of the world, including the U.S., is one factor in the increase in the size of children. The NIH also reports that, "Japanese children born after World War II are consuming a diet richer in protein by 20 percent. When they reach school, these children can no longer fit into the school desks used by their parents."

The racks of cookbooks and books on nutrition that threaten to engulf our bookstores and libraries today will advise you at great length on what foods supply the body with protein. The main object is to consume the essential amino acid components of protein that the body can't manufacture for itself. Each species of plant and animal has its unique set of protein, made up of various amino acids linked together in different sequences. According to nutritionists, the food an adult human being eats must provide eight certain amino acids, called the essential amino acids. A child needs a diet with a ninth amino acid, histidine. A normally functioning body utilizes these essential amino acids to make additional ones, so that a total of 23 different amino acids are available for use as the basic building blocks of all the different proteins in the body. All of these amino acids are different chemical arrangements of the elements carbon, hydrogen, nitrogen and oxygen, and sometimes traces of other elements. By the process of transcription we discussed in chapter 2, the DNA structure of the genes in the cell nucleus dictates which proteins are metabolized by each cell. But no growth is possible, neither new growth in children nor renewed growth in adults, without the intake, every day, of foods containing the essential amino acids.

VITAMINS AND MINERALS

I've compiled a concise list of the vitamins and minerals that are particularly associated with the process of linear growth, including a few brief notes on what they do, and what foods supply them. Of course all the many vitamins and minerals that a body utilizes are essential raw materials in the total building program, and a lack of any one can affect overall health and growth.

You might like to keep in mind that vitamins are chemical compounds that serve as catalysts with the enzymes to assist in all the reactions that occur in your body's chemical factory. Minerals become part of new compounds that form structural components of your body. Although essential, their quantity in the body is very slight, some in such minute amounts that only recent advances in measuring techniques have revealed their presence.

First, the vitamins:

VITAMIN A

More commonly known to cause night blindness, a deficiency of vitamin A also thickens the long bones of a growing child and leads to growth retardation. Vitamin A is required in the bone-building process to allow old bone to be absorbed in proper proportion to the laying down of new bone. Remember from chapter 2 that this process occurs throughout life, but is of primary importance in childhood to the development of a person's height. The *minimum* daily requirement increases as a child gets older, with the adult level now established at 5,000 units a day, or one and a half milligrams.

The main source of this vitamin is liver and the yellow or orange pigments called carotenes found in carrots and other plants and fruits. Recently scientists are finding that excess intake can also stunt growth. When bone modeling is speeded up the result is a weakening of the bone, a proneness to fracture, and sometimes abnormal growths on the bones.

VITAMIN C

Nutritionists' opinions conflict as to how much of this important vitamin we need every day, but they agree it's easy to obtain through many fruits and leafy green vegetables. Without vitamin C the cells cannot make healthy soft tissues, including cartilage and the matrix of bone. If these tissues are abnormal or weak, the process of calcification goes awry and bones do not grow normally.

VITAMIN D

Two of the main building blocks of growing bones are calcium and phosphorus, and Vitamin D is indispensable in the process of absorbing both minerals from food in the intestines. Vitamin D is formed by cells in our skin when it's exposed to the sun, so it's nicknamed the sunshine vitamin. Without it the bones can't mineralize properly, and then grow soft and bowed, in a disease called rickets. For centuries rickets was a problem, particularly in cold, cloudy northern climates. Since the 1930's, vitamin D has been added to milk, which also supplies calcium, phosphorus and vitamin A, so milk drinkers get all the important bone builders at the same time. Only a tiny amount is needed—400 units a day, which is ten millionths of a gram (and a gram is one twenty-eighth of an ounce). But not getting that amount causes softening of the bones in adults as well as children. Cheese is a good milk substitute and fish oils are another source of vitamin D . . . a dose of cod liver oil was the old-fashioned remedy.

Vitamin D not only increases the absorption of calcium from food, it also increases resorption of calcium in the bone-modeling process. Both actions raise the level of calcium in the blood, permitting normal activity of nerves and muscles (see chapter 2).

Some children have a lowered response to vitamin D, and even when they receive adequate amounts in their diet their bodies react as though there's a deficiency. The most common form of this disorder is an inherited disease called vitamin D-resistant rickets.

Like many necessary nutrients, if consumed in too large amounts vitamin D becomes a poison. It raises the blood serum calcium level too much and causes calcification of soft tissues, such as the kidneys.

Now the minerals:

CALCIUM AND PHOSPHORUS

No healthy growth occurs without these minerals, and their combination in calcium phosphate forms the hardness of bone structure on which our heights depend. Calcium makes up two percent of the body weight and phosphorus one percent. They are both readily available in milk as noted above, and also in cheese.

ZINC

The body's need for this mineral was established in the 1960's when doctors in Europe and the Middle East discovered that one disease characterized by dwarfism, among other symptoms, could be cured by zinc supplements. Apparently zinc is required for the proper functioning of many different enzymes. The best source is animal products.

POTASSIUM

A partial deficiency causes slow growth. An essential trace mineral for many body functions, potassium is found widely in foods, particularly green leaves, but, like many nutrients, is easily lost when foods are refined or when vegetable-cooking water is discarded.

MANGANESE, MAGNESIUM, COPPER, FLUORINE

Elements required in trace amounts for the normal formation of bone.

Before we leave the subject of vitamins and minerals, I want to make a couple of comments. First, I'm being very unfair to the wondrously coordinated chemical factory of our bodies to isolate these nutrients. My purpose is to point out that a person will not reach his tallest height potential if he's deficient in any one of them. However, please keep in mind that they don't function individually. As the well-known nutritionist Adelle Davis wrote in *Let's Eat Right to Keep Fit,* "Every nutrient has its own duties; yet each works cooperatively with the others. Vitamin E helps linoleic acid, linoleic acid helps vitamin D, vitamin D helps phosphorus, phosphorus helps calcium, calcium helps vitamin C, ad infinitum. No nutrient plays a hermit role."

Secondly, scientists are gathering increasing proof that often too much of these nutrients can cause as much damage as too little. Physicians talk of "wisdom of the body" to excrete what it can't use, but, as Joseph Samachson points out in his book *The Armor Within Us,* "this wisdom depends on the chemical and nerve signals that the digestive tract and the kidneys receive, and once these signals go wrong, the body may act quite stupidly."

Whether you add vitamin and mineral supplements to your family's diet is up to you and your doctor. Many scientists believe that the wholesale use of vitamin pills in recent decades has been partly responsible for the fact that the current generation of Americans is taller and heavier than previous generations.

Sugar

As I mentioned in the previous chapter, the ingestion of sugar shuts off secretion of HGH from the pituitary gland. However, if stuffing ourselves with sweets affected the overall function of growth hormone, all Americans would have been midgets by now at the rate our sugar consumption has increased. But why take chances with your children's growth? I say, give HGH a chance and don't work insulin overtime.

Prenatal and Infant Nutrition

Although babies born in starving areas of the world are smaller than the average American newborn, it is usually caused by chronic malnutrition of the mother since childhood rather than a deficiency only during pregnancy. The baby takes what it needs for growth from the mother, even if it means depleting the mother's stores and depriving her body of essential nutrients. How many of you mothers (besides me!) developed cavities in your teeth during pregnancy because your baby was robbing you of calcium?

When my children were born in the early '60's it was still the vogue for doctors to restrict pregnant moms to a gain of no more than 20 pounds in order to limit the size of the baby, thereby promoting an easier delivery. But doctors now know that limiting a mother's weight gain does not materially reduce the size of the baby. However, as we discussed earlier, there are many factors that do influence the size of the newborn. Some of these factors the mother can control, such as smoking, drinking, and drug consumption, and some she can't, such as illness and placental infection, or perhaps a twin not competing successfully for its share of the nutrients (the "runt" effect). I highly recommend the new book *Caring For Your Unborn Child,* by Drs. Barbara and Ronald Gots, for a complete summary of these important factors.

The newborn infant receives, in appropriate quantities, all the protein and calories it needs in the milk supplied by an adequately nourished mother. In fact, even the milk of a malnourished mother provides the basic nutrients. The babies suffering from marasmus and kwashiorkor in developing nations do not usually begin to be ill until after the weaning process. But HEW studies show that in the U.S. low-income mothers seldom breast feed, and so the malnourishment of the children often begins at birth. Therefore the victims of maramus and kwashiorkor in our country may prove to be more severely retarded in growth than in the poorest countries in the world.

Two more points about the advantages of human milk that have recently come to light concern specific ingredients essential to growth that are not found in cow's milk. According to the NIH, a new study has disclosed that a premature baby may lack the ability to manufacture cystine, which is one of the 23 amino acids that a fully developed human can make for itself. Human milk has a high cystine content and therefore helps the premature baby develop until it can manufacture its own. Some scientists blame the tendency of many premature infants to develop short height and mental deficiency on the lack of cystine. In fact, one inherited illness called homocystinuria, in which a person is unable to manufacture cystine from other amino acids, results in a similar pattern of stunted growth and mental retardation.

Secondly, doctors at Massachusetts General Hospital have announced that mother's milk appears to give some protection to infants born with a lack of thyroid hormone. The report said that, "We have conducted studies which indicate that human breast milk contains sufficient thyroid hormone to lessen congenital hypothyroidism and possibly prevent impaired neurological development." The mother's milk appears to block the disease's development long enough to prevent the damaging effects of cretinism before therapy is begun.

Many studies indicate that nature does her best to provide our babies with every essential nutrient for growth from conception through weaning. After that it's up to us to carry the ball. Few American youngsters starve to death, but there is much concern over the long-term effects of even slight nutritional deficiencies.

Growth Rates of Girls and Boys

The National Institutes of Health book on *How Children Grow* states: "Nutritionists are looking into the possibility that the growth differences between boys and girls may require that the two sexes be put on different diets right from birth." Does that surprise you? Not only do the sexes grow at different rates, but the very nature of growth itself may differ so much that the required nutrients vary. For example, take muscle cells. Boys and girls are probably born with the same number and size of muscle cells. According to the NIH report, by 3 weeks of age boys already have more muscle cells than girls. At about age 10 a girl will have about five times as many muscle cells as when she was born, and little further increase occurs in either number or size. But boys' muscle cells continue to multiply until at 18 years he has at least 14 times as many as he had at birth and they may continue to enlarge for another 5 years. Once muscle cells stop growing, further enlargement of the muscle is due to increasing the diameter of the fibrils contained inside the muscle cells.

In addition to their radically changing biological status during adolescence, the differing attitudes of boys and girls toward weight gain affects their nutritional condition, which in turn may affect their growth. Most teenage boys welcome the weight gain at this time in their lives. It's a positive sign of growing taller and stronger. Girls in our society, on the other hand, desire only to be slender, and the natural weight increase caused by those maturing female fat deposits is not welcome at all. Thus begin fanatical diets that often result in malnutrition. Teenage girls are one of our largest categories of malnourished Americans. As NIH points out, even overweight girls who consume excessive amounts of calories are also frequently inadequate nutritionally.

Scientists have discovered that a girl has more fatty tissue right from birth than a boy of equal age and size. Because of these fat reserves, a girl's caloric needs throughout life are pound for pound less than her brother's. In addition, a girl is biologically more mature than a boy from birth and her physical development is more stable. Growth studies sponsored by NIH have also indicated that when exposed to growth-retarding illnesses, a boy is much more adversely affected than a girl. However, once the condition is treated, a boy usually recovers from the lag with faster catchup growth.

OBESITY

Too much of anything is a bad thing, and so it goes with food and growth. For one thing, obesity seems to retard the secretion of growth hormone. One of our many eminent scientists studying this problem, Dr. Willard VanderLaan of Scripps Clinic, said at the NPA symposium, "One of the earliest observations on anomalies of GH secretion . . . was that obesity was associated with low plasma concentration and blunted responses were found to standard stimuli for secretion."

As any TV comedian will remind you, a big chunk of our society is short and fat, including children. The question is, are they short because they're fat or fat because they're short?

Many studies are concentrating on the effects of obesity on growth and health, from birth to death. The NIH report that about 8 percent of youngsters in affluent nations are being overfed. Infants regulate their food intake by volume, and some scientists believe that formulas overly rich in calories and protein may be stimulating the formation of excess fat cells that can never disappear through either time or diet.

Overnutrition speeds up the growth and maturation process. In his paper, "Body Size and Implications," anthropologist Stanley M. Garn notes, "Menarche is earlier in fatter girls, in some cases by two or three years or more . . . Fat children are more mature and bigger earlier . . . but they stop growing sooner." As Garn and others point out, and as we noted in chapter 3, improved nutrition is one of the major factors underlying the increase in average height during the last century. However, improved nutrition has also led to obesity which leads to a whole myriad of health problems. Garn adds, "We have begun to wonder whether greater body size and earlier maturation has been purchased at the expense of predisposition to cardiovascular and atherosclerotic diseases."

Malabsorption

Sometimes children's normal growth processes are disturbed not because of inadequate diet but rather because of some inability of the body to digest and absorb nutrients. For example, according to the NIH, 70 percent of American black people lack a digestive enzyme needed to convert the sugar in cow's milk to a kind that can be absorbed. Scientists have developed soybean and other non-milk formulas for affected newborns.

Dr. Blizzard tells parents that if a child has large, foul, bulky stools and any other abdominal symptoms, he should be checked for poor absorption of food substances.

In cases of malabsorption as well as most other illnesses that retard growth, the stunted child shows almost magical powers of growth once the illness has been treated successfully. For example, a child whose too-narrow artery between heart and lung was surgically widened grew the equivalent of 4 years in bone age during 6 months, bringing him near the same point he would have reached had he never suffered the defect. In another case reported by NIH a 4-year-old girl had a tumor removed from her adrenal glands and grew at the rate of a six-month-old baby until she caught up to her normal height-for-age. Scientists have so far been unable to explain this catchup phenomenon, but in almost all cases a slowdown occurs after the catchup spurt, and growth doesn't overshoot the mark. The earlier the underlying illness is treated, the faster the catchup growth. In later childhood or puberty, catchup growth is slower and the child is less likely to reach full potential height. This same catchup spurt is demonstrated when hormone deficiencies are corrected, as in hypopituitarism or hypothyroidism.

The tremendous decrease in childhood diseases affecting

Emotion

Drinking from toilet bowls. Eating dog food. Stealing food from neighbors. Raiding the refrigerator and eating the whole jar of mustard or mayonnaise. Weird? Bizarre? Yes. But this behavior is becoming a familiar story to many pediatricians, especially Dr. Robert Blizzard, who first studied and described the causes of these symptoms. One of these cases, reported in *Medical World News,* was that of a little four-year-old girl. When Margie was brought to Dr. Blizzard, he was concerned about her obviously stunted growth, in addition to her bizarre behavior. She was 35¼ inches tall, the length of a 28-month-old baby, and her bone age was 2 to 2½. At 25 pounds she was 5 pounds underweight for her stunted height, in spite of her voracious feeding habits. Margie's immediate need was treatment of a facial gash, which required 22 stitches. Margie never whimpered and seemed indifferent to pain.

Dr. Blizzard learned that when Margie was 14 months old she had watched her mother being shot dead by an ex-boyfriend. Since that time, her treatment by her father and stepmother had alternated between neglect and abuse.

After only 4 days in the hospital Margie had gained 5 pounds and her height began shooting up like the fabled beanstalk.

Dr. Blizzard studied 13 patients like Margie in the early 1960's and established a diagnosis which relates emotions to growth. Margie was one of many emotionally battered children with stunted growth, a problem now called psychosocial short stature. Doctors believe that severe maltreatment of emotional neglect in the home environment is a far more frequent cause of growth failure than can be proved. Parents who neglect their children usually don't take them to doctors, so these children can only be helped by neighbors, other relatives, social workers, or others.

Why do these children stop growing? Apparently emotional

trauma shuts off the production of growth hormone.

In many cases studied by Dr. Blizzard, Dr. Raiti and others, the patients found to be deficient in HGH showed other symptoms of hypopituitarism. Dr. Raiti recalls that when this situation was first discovered, HGH was not available for treatment, but because of the home problems the children were placed in foster homes. "To our surprise, we found that these kids started to grow," Dr. Raiti said. "When we tested them after six months, we found they were producing growth hormone. A couple of them went back to their homes and stopped growing; they stopped making HGH."

When these unloved children are removed from the problems at home, their catchup growth rate is usually dramatic. In a case reported at Cornell Medical Center, a 6-year-old boy, who was the height of a 2-year-old when he arrived at the hospital, at one point was growing at the equivalent rate of 12 inches a year. He was given no HGH or other growth-inducing medication. When Joey was sent back to his emotionally-disturbed mother he stopped growing again, so he was placed in a happy, loving foster home, where he continued his catchup spurt.

Many doctors think that improved growth in these situations is caused by improved nutrition. Recent investigations are proving that the functioning of the digestive system is very susceptible to emotional states. Doctors now know that the absorption of calcium, for example, is affected by anxiety, which only proves what people have known for centuries: the importance of eating in pleasant surroundings and in a relaxed frame of mind. So when emotionally deprived children are nourished in a happier atmosphere, their food is better absorbed and utilized, encouraging growth. However, testing of HGH levels indicates that improved nutrition is not the only factor controlling the catchup growth spurt.

In emotionally deprived environments, children often lack adequate sleep, and as I mentioned in discussing HGH, a substantial amount of the body's growth-hormone supply is secreted during deep sleep. Research studies show that children grow less in times of fitful sleep compared to periods of peaceful rest, but the direct mechanism has not been pinpointed. Physicians prefer to list sleeplessness as a symptom of emotional problems rather than a cause of stunted growth.

Remember in the previous chapter I mentioned the connection between the pituitary gland and the hypothalamus? The two are joined by blood vessels and nerves, and current research has so far revealed at least one specific factor (somatostatin) from the hypothalamus controlling release of HGH from the pituitary. This area at the base of the brain is under intense scientific scrutiny as it appears to be the area where unconscious activities are initiated. The hypothalamus is controlled by higher centers in the nervous system, which are in turn controlled by the cerebral cortex, the portion of the brain responsible for conscious thought. If scientists can learn how the cerebral cortex controls the hypothalamus, perhaps they will learn how basic body processes like growth are influenced by emotions.

Psychosocial short stature indicates that severe emotional problems can directly affect growth. Whether minor ones can remains to be proved by continuing research. However, all the evidence so far underscores the importance of what wise mothers have known for centuries: give your children plenty of good food, sleep, exercise and lots of love. And a pinch to grow an inch can't hurt. Then they will grow "sooo big."

6 Genetics and Height

> *Every man must do his own growing no matter how tall his grandfather was.*
>
> Anon.

Short people seem to be crawling out of the woodwork lately—have you noticed? Gary Player has won three top golf tournaments and Richard Dreyfuss captured the Best Actor Oscar, and they're both short. In fact, when you consider the whole category of actors, there are many successful ones who aren't exactly tall—Paul Newman and Robert Redford, for example, and Dustin Hoffman. Situation comedies on TV are spoofing the problems of short adolescent boys: "James at 16" agonized through his crush on a tall girl who called him "short ribs," and last night a new show introduced a cute little guy who finally got up his nerve to ask "the giraffe" for a date.

Everyone who hears about this book confides in almost confessional tones that they are short too, or they had a child or a friend or a neighbor who is short. I wrote to request photos from Ringling Bros.-Barnum & Bailey Circus, and in his response, their public relations man added, "By the way, I'm only 5'5"." I talked long distance to Terry Cole at the NPA about pituitary-gland collection, and he inserted into the conversation, "By the way, I'm only 5'6"." My neighbor told me her boss is 5'4". The real estate agent we bought a house from has a daughter 5'1", and Linda's school counselor has a daughter 5 feet. And so on.

There's a whole army of us short people who have normally functioning hormones, adequate nutrition, a healthy childhood environment, and no malformation of our bones. Like the old saying, we walk, we talk, we're almost human! Why are we short? Because we inherited short stature from our parents.

Now, let's be careful here. If you are short and if you are reading this book because you are concerned about the short height of your children, don't just say, "Oh well, they inherited short genes and there's nothing I can do about that!" and sweep the whole subject under the rug. First, following the guidelines I suggested in preceeding chapters, make sure that your children's short stature isn't complicated by problems that may exist in addition to the inherited tendency to be short. Second, there is plenty you can do to help your short children psychologically (see chapter 8), even if their physical development is as normal as their genes allow.

I think that many people consider their biological inheritance as inevitable and uncontrollable as death and taxes, and also as mysterious and difficult to understand, so it's pushed out of mind. All that business about genes and chromosomes and dominant and recessive and X and Y and meiosis and autosomes and phonotype and genotype . . . yes, it was confusing in high school biology and it still is. Why bother? Well, for one reason because understanding the process of heredity will help you understand who and what you are, not only your short height but your red hair, your freckled face, and your tendency toward cancer and heart disease. Another reason is because many kinds of short stature are inherited, both normal and abnormal varieties. So let's dig into the topic of genetics, and I'll try to make it more interesting than taxes and less mysterious than death.

Chromosomes, genes, and DNA were explained briefly in chapter 2 in the discussion of how a body grows, but let's review. Chromosomes are long threads of material within every cell nucleus. Human beings have 46 chromosomes in each cell, arranged in 23 pairs, which are identically duplicated every time a cell divides in the process called mitosis. The chemical composition of the chromosomes is the ladder-like, double-helix structure of DNA. We discussed how DNA "unzips" to reproduce itself in mitosis and also to transfer its instructions concerning protein synthesis to the cell, thereby directing all activities of a living organism. The unique arrangement of the rungs of the DNA ladders that compose each organism's chromosomes is the "genetic code." Sections of a DNA strip in a chromosome that control different pieces of information in the code are called genes. A gene may consist of perhaps 500 to 2,000 rungs of the DNA ladder—no one knows how many, nor how many different genes a human cell contains. Estimates range from as low as a total of 10,000 genes for all the chromosomes to as high as 20,000 for each individual chromosome.

Two of the 46 chromosomes (one pair) carry the directions that dictate whether the person will be male or female, and so are called sex chromosomes. The other 44, called autosomes, also occur in pairs and direct the rest of life's processes. So there are 23 pairs of chromosomes in each cell, and somewhere in those miles of threadlike DNA are coded instructions that tell your cells how tall you are capable of growing.

But not all human cells have 23 pairs of chromosomes. The reproductive cells, the egg and the sperm, each have 23—period—one chromosome from each pair. When they join in conception the new organism has the required complement of 23 pairs, and this genetic code raps out the instructions for the development of a new human being.

How do the reproductive cells end up with only a half share of chromosomes? This tricky process, called meiosis, is the basis of reproduction and also explains how you inherit half your genes from your father and half from your mother.

Although the egg and sperm aren't functional until puberty, their formation begins in the development of the embryo long before birth. About the end of the first month of prenatal life, in the mass of developing tissue, there occurs a special cell called a germ cell. The germ cells begin reproducing themselves and gradually move to the site of the developing reproductive organs. In the female, by about the third month after conception there are hundreds of thousands of germ cells concentrated in the ovaries. These cells now gradually change into forerunners of the ova, or eggs, called primary oocytes. The process of oogenesis takes place in three stages. In simplified terms, it goes like this:

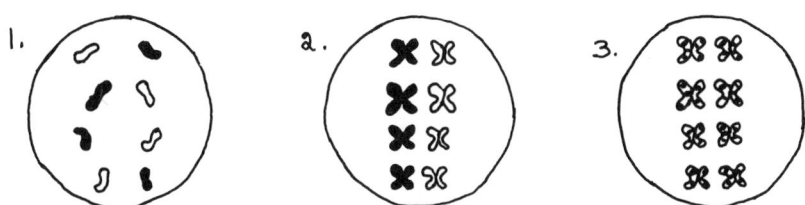

Fig. 14. (1) Female germ cell nucleus with 23 pairs of chromosomes (4 pairs are shown here for simplicity, with black representing those from the mother and white those from the father.) (2) Chromosomes pair up and each reproduces itself, the two strands staying attached at their centers. The matched, doubled pairs line up at cell center with each chromosomes from the unborn baby's father lying parallel to a chromosome from the mother. (3) Then apparently some of the sections of the chromosomes, genes, that are exactly opposite each other, change place by a process called crossing over, integrating the genes from both mother and father and increasing the infinite variety of the genetic jigsaw puzzle.

At this point, the process in the female stops. And she isn't even born yet! About seven million of these oocytes are packed into her ovaries by about the fifth prenatal month, and there they rest until the female's childbearing years from puberty to menopause. As Virginia Apgar and Joan Beck point out in their excellent book *Is My Baby All Right?:* "During this long waiting period, hundreds of thousands of the oocytes disintegrate and disappear. By birth, only about two million are still in existence and by the age of seven, all but 300,000 to 500,000 are gone. Only 350 to 400 will ever mature into fully developed eggs, or ova. By the age of 45 to 55, all of them will have disappeared."

When the process of cell division resumes in the ovary, it's called meiosis and it proceeds in two stages transforming the oocyte to an ovum:

1. FIRST MEIOTIC DIVISION

2. SECOND MEIOTIC DIVISION

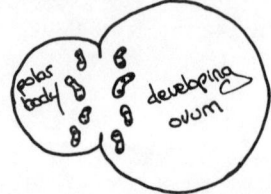

Fig. 15. (1) The pairs of chromosomes pull apart during cell division so that 23 entire doubled chromosomes go into each new cell. Some were originally from the mother and some from the father, but all contain some of the cross-over genes. One of the new cells keeps most of the cytoplasm from the original cell. The second cell is called a polar body and soon disintegrates. (2) Now the developing ovum divides again. This time 23 doubled chromosomes separate so that each new cell has one each of the 23 chromosomes. Once again most of the cytoplasm stays with one of the new cells, and the second cell (another polar body) disintegrates. In this fashion one germ cell produces one mature ovum with its proper share of 23 chromosomes and lots of cytoplasm to nourish the fertilized egg.

The cell-division process that forms the male sperm works the same way except that the whole process from germ cell to sperm, incorporating all five steps outlined above, does not begin until puberty. During meiosis the cytoplasm divides equally so that four sperm result from one germ cell. In other words, there are no polar bodies that disintegrate as in the drawings above. The first meiotic division produces two equal cells with one doubled chromosome from each pair, and in the second meiotic division both of those cells divide again to produce four sperm cells, each with 23 single chromosomes.

One of the other major differences in male meiosis occurs in the lining up of the pair of sex chromosomes called X and Y. Females have two X chromosomes and males have one X and one Y. The presence of the Y chromosomes makes a male. During meiosis in the male, the X and Y chromosomes line up and double but do not cross over any genes. The doubled X chromosome (inherited from the mother) will end up in two sperm, and all the genes those X chromosomes carry in addition to the female sex characteristics are passed along unchanged. If one of those X sperm penetrate the egg, it's a girl. On the other hand, the doubled Y chromosome ends up in 2 Y sperm, which apparently carry only the genes determining male sex. If one of the Y sperm penetrates the egg, it's a boy.

In males, the full cycle of spermatogenesis takes about 64 days, whereas oogenesis begins in prenatal life and takes 12 to 50 years to complete. The supply of sperm seems almost unlimited. A single ejaculation discharges an estimated 200 million to 500 million sperm! The germ cells begin sperm production in early adolescence and continue producing fresh sperm as long as disease, accident, or old age don't interfere.

Do you understand how each fertilized egg begins with half of its genetic material from the father and half from the mother and how the genetic material on each of the 23 pairs of chromosomes is resorted and distributed from generation to generation?

The next point to understand in this matter of heredity is that the paired chromosomes contain genes that more or less control the same body function. For an extremely simplified example, think of one chromosome pair and say that one gene from each chromosome in this pair dictates blood type. Remember, one of these chromosomes is from the mother and the other from the father and they paired up at conception. So two genes dictate for blood type. Which one rules? Although some genes apparently cooperate together, most genes obey Mendel's laws and follow a dominant-recessive pattern. In other words, all genes aren't created equal. In the case of blood type, geneticists have learned that blood type A is dominant and blood type O is recessive. If you inherit one gene for type A and one gene for type O, your blood type is A. For a recessive gene to govern there must be two recessives, so all people with type O blood inherited two type O genes. People with type A blood might have two type A genes or one A and one O.

Say you are type A and your 2 blood-type genes are A and O. Each of your children has a 50-50 chance of receiving one or the other of those 2 genes from you. But that doesn't mean that half your children will get one gene and half get the other gene. Every time you toss a coin there's a 50% chance of it falling heads and 50% tails. If you toss it up 4 times, it won't necessarily fall heads twice and tails twice—it may fall heads all 4 times, because each time you toss it up in the air there's a fresh 50-50 chance. It works the same way with your genes. If you have four children they may all have inherited the gene for type O blood from you. By the same token, if you're a man, your X and Y sex chromosomes divide equally into your sperm cells, and each of your children has a 50-50 chance of receiving the X (a girl) or the Y (a boy).

Often it is not just a single pair of genes that control one characteristic, but a combination of genes. Height is an example. As we've discussed, stature is the end result of many body functions, including the entire body's ability to multiply and enlarge its cells as well as the particular function of the skeletal and endocrine systems. Therefore many, many genes are involved. But still, it's obvious that most tall parents have tall kids and short parents have short kids—or, as Dr. Blizzard phrases it, Great Danes produce Great Danes and Scotty dogs give birth to Scotty dogs.

Our genes dictate our height potential—how long our bones will grow, how our cells respond to hormones, etc. With each pair of the thousands of genes operating in conjunction or according to the dominant-recessive rules, all the genetic decisions about your growth are made at microscopic level. Then the action of the genes is influenced by their environment of the cell, which is acted on by its environment of the tissue, which is under orders of the rest of the body, which must react to the whole environment around it. It's like the "cat's cradle"—a very complex whole, but pull one string and it all falls apart.

Until this century, stature was considered strictly a racial characteristic inherited within a group of people and passed on from generation to generation, uninfluenced by environment. The Pygmies and Watusis, the shortest and tallest population groups in the world, seemed to prove this theory.

Pygmy groups live in Africa and Southeast Asia. The short tribes in Africa, called Negrillos, average about four and a half feet in height, whereas the groups in Asia, called Negritos, are slightly taller. Although they are all short with dark skin and wooly hair, these two groups are apparently unrelated to each other, although some anthropologists believe they stem from the same original stock. Pygmies are a very ancient people; they are depicted in Egyptian drawings 4,000 years old.

Recently an excellent program on educational TV, "Children of the Forest," showed the lives of Zaire's Mbuti Pygmies. Numbering about 40,000, these nomadic hunters enjoy more protein than most people in Africa. Although some girls marry outside their villages, few Mbuti men take wives from the outside, so their breeding is mostly contained within the group. Recent blood-typing tests show that the Mbuti are a more distinct and more ancient population than most other African groups. They are a peaceful people who hunt throughout the 50,000 square miles of the Ituri Forest. They have the ability to run great distances following their prey, and the highest achievement is killing an elephant. Their future is threatened by a government that's attempting to make them stay in roadside settlements, where they die of heat stroke and dysentery.

As I watched these happy people so well adapted to their forest life, two features seemed obvious to me. First, that without any taller people to compare them to, they didn't appear short at all. The environment they created for themselves, their homes and tools and weapons, were suited to their size. No cupboards they can't reach, no cars they can't drive. If I could have asked them if it bothered them to be short, they probably would have thought I was nuts—a crazy, weird female with red hair and white skin (but I bet they wouldn't think I'm short!) The other aspect of their lives that I pondered was the influence of their size on their life style and vice versa. Doesn't being small help them run silently and swiftly through the thick forest?

Explanations of why pygmies don't grow taller are being researched. No deficiency of growth hormone or somatomedin has been found, but studies suggest that pygmies' HGH may have reduced biological activity, or that some defect prevents their bodies from responding to normal stimuli.

Not far from the Mbuti live the world's tallest people, the Watusi. Averaging about six and a half feet, the Watusi and other tall African tribes are also very thin. Living out in the open rather than in the forest, their dark-skinned, long bodies have more surface area to dissipate the equatorial heat. Mainly cattle-herders, the Nilotic tribes keep thin on their high-protein milk and meat diet. Like the pygmies, these tall tribes rarely interbreed with outsiders, so their genetic inheritance encourages a consistent stature from generation to generation. Since both the tall and the short live in the same corner of the world, environment may seem to have little influence on their stature. But closer study reveals that it is the subtle interplay of both genetics and environment that determines height in all peoples of the world, even the tallest and shortest.

Anthropologists have attempted to categorize taller and heavier population groups with northern, colder climates and to place smaller people closer to the equator. This works for tall Swedes and short Italians, but there are so many exceptions, such as the Watusi, that general categories are almost meaningless. In addition, rarely do different groups express a specific height consistently. There are short Swedes and tall Italians. As anthropologist Stephen Molnar points out in his book, *Races, Types and Ethnic Groups,* "Seldom do we appreciate that the range of man's diversity extends in gradual degrees throughout the species."

As the world's population becomes more mobile, interbreeding has become more evident and a more influential factor in our evolution. When the genes for "tallness" combine with the genes for "shortness," the resulting compromise would appear to bring us all closer and closer to our species' "ideal" height, whatever that is. As expert geneticist Victor McKusick states in his well-known text, *Human Genetics,* "Man is all one species with no chromosomal differences between the various races and with free interbreeding possible." However, scientists usually agree that even if we had total integration of all the different races and population groups, the interwoven reactions between heredity and environment would still produce perfectly normal short people and tall people. One reason is because we measure these extremes in mere inches. After all, even the average Mbuti and Watusi differ by only two feet, only two-thirds of a yardstick. Consider the comparisons in other species, a Mexican Chihuahua and St. Bernard, for instance, or a Shetland pony and a Clydesdale.

In our American culture, where bigger is supposedly better and small people often get the short end of the stick, there are millions of people who are considered short even though their genetic makeups are within normal limits. There are also thousands of people who are short because of some defect in the genetic structure that they inherited from their parents.

Some recessive genes pass from generation to generation for centuries without affecting anyone because they're so rare that they're seldom mated with the same recessive, and their opposite dominant gene overrules them. Geneticists estimate that each of us carries 2–8 recessive genes potentially lethal to a baby if joined with a like recessive. Many birth defects are caused by the pairing up of abnormal recessive genes, some occurring more frequently than others and some more harmful than others.

Sometimes hypopituitarism is caused by inheriting two defective recessive genes. A paper by Victor McKusick, of Johns Hopkins, and David Rimoin of Los Angeles's Harbor General Hospital, two of the leading physicians specializing in short stature, revealed that the midget builds of 3'2" Charles Stratton, better known as General Tom Thumb, and his wife, 2'8" Lavinia Bump, were caused by the inherited recessive genes which resulted in a lack of growth hormone. Both of their parents were of normal size, indicating that they must have carried the normal dominant gene as well as the recessive one. Significantly, however, Tom Thumb's parents were first cousins and Lavinia's parents were third cousins. When a single defective gene exists in a family tree, and members of that family intermarry, the chances of one offspring inheriting two of the abnormal recessive genes is much greater than when members of the family mate outside into a wider gene pool.

McKusick and Rimoin studied several short-statured couples with isolated growth hormone deficiency and their children, who also inherited the recessive genes. All children of midget mothers must be delivered by Caesarean section as their babies are of normal size at birth. Thus it appears that prenatal growth is not controlled by growth hormone from either mother or fetus. They couldn't draw any conclusions from their study as to how the biological mechanism resulting in lack of HGH works. It may be that the defective genes prevent production of the hormone, or perhaps they produce an inactive molecule. The defect may also lie somewhere in the intricate pathways of the hypothalamus' signals to the pituitary.

McKusick and Rimoin also report that although panhypopituitarism (when all hormones from the anterior pituitary lobe are deficient) is not usually an inherited problem, they did find some rare inherited cases. They studied an inbred group of Hutterites, a religious sect of people living communally in some parts of the plains areas in Canada and the U.S. It is evident that inbred families have a much greater chance of producing children with severe abnormalities caused by defective recessive genes than the rest of the population.

This effect has also been noted in a group of Amish living in Pennsylvania, who contain in unprecedented frequency a particular form of dwarfism accompanied by extra fingers (polydactyly). McKusick reports in *Human Genetics* that the 8,000 members of this group descend from three couples who came to America before 1770, and one of them must have carried the defective gene. Through inbreeding, sixty-one cases of dwarfism-polydactyly have been found among this Amish group, whereas only 50 other cases have been reported in all of medical literature.

For any recessive trait to show up, both parents must carry the recessive gene, even if its effect is masked by a dominant gene. When two normal parents both carry recessive defective genes, there is one chance out of four that a child will inherit both defective genes and consequently have the abnormality. (See diagram, Figure 16)

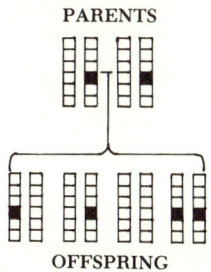

Fig. 16. Recessive Inheritance. These diagramatic chromosomes show how a recessive gene (black), paired with a dominant gene *(white)* in both parents *(top)*, could be combined in their offspring *(bottom)*. There is a 50% chance, or two out of four, that the recessive gene would be paired with the dominant gene and not have any effect on the child *(first and second from left)*. There is a 25% chance, or one out of four, that the child would not inherit the recessive gene at all, but instead have both dominant genes *(third from left)*. There is also a 25% chance that the child will inherit both recessive genes *(right)*, which would give rise to the recessive trait.

When defects are caused by a dominant gene, only one parent need have the disorder. In such a case, there is one chance in two that the abnormal gene will be passed on to every child, even if the matching gene inherited from the other parent is normal. If one parent has a set of two defective dominant genes, every child will inherit the defect. Dominant inheritance patterns are easier to trace than recessive because their effects are usually obvious.

How do genes become defective? Many changes in the genetic makeup of *homo sapiens* have taken place over the centuries. Gradual advantageous change is, indeed, evolution. But some changes called mutations occur suddenly. Most of them are apparently the spontaneous result of natural cosmic radiation and chemicals in the earth to which all living matter is exposed. A dangerous side effect to this century of scientific progress has been increased exposure to radiation from X-rays and atomic energy and to a multitude of drugs. It's difficult for scientists to measure the damage because defects may not show up for generations.

Mutations can affect both the body cells and the germ cells and are duplicated by both mitosis and meiosis. When the germ cells are affected, the mutated genes are passed along through egg or sperm. Now that the effects of X-rays are more clearly understood, the dosage is minimized whenever possible, especially to the reproductive organs. Scientists have roughly estimated that an accumulated dose of 45–100 rads (units of absorbed radiation) would produce twice the number of genetic mutations as occur spontaneously. For comparison, 5 rads are about the amount a body receives in full barium X-rays.

In the laboratory, mutations of single genes have been caused by many chemical substances, but it is difficult for scientists to obtain definite proof of the affect of these chemicals on humans, as they can't use us as they do mice. However, many drugs, LSD for example, have been strongly implicated as causing mutations to germ cells that affect future generations.

When a birth defect is caused by the pregnant mother taking drugs or becoming ill, the malformation is not considered to be inherited even though the baby is born with it. The prenatal environment is to blame, not the genetic material inherited from the parents. The drug thalidamide, which caused the epidemic of phocomelia (malformation of arms and legs) in the early 1960's, and German measles, which was also discovered in the 1960's to affect unborn children with various severe abnormalities, are two prime examples of causes of birth defects in this category. It's important to understand that all problems present at birth are not inherited from the parents and will not necessarily be a part of the child's genetic makeup, to be passed on to his children.

In addition to defective single genes, abnormalities can also involve several genes or segments of chromosomes, or even whole chromosomes. During the long process of meiosis, from the time the germ cells are first formed in the embryo until the mature egg or sperm is finally utilized after puberty, there is plenty of opportunity for something to foul up the delicate business of crossing-over, duplication and cell division. Maybe bits of chromosome get destroyed or broken apart and rejoined in the wrong order. Maybe instead of 23 chromosomes the cell ends up with 22 or 24.

Scientists estimate that half of all fertilized eggs are lost early in pregnancy because of chromosome abnormalities that are incompatible with life. One-half of one percent survive and the baby is born with severe abnormalities.

Techniques for counting and identifying the 23 pairs of chromosomes weren't perfected until 1956, and in 1959 the cause of Down's syndrome (mongolism) was pinpointed as an extra chromosome. Mongoloids have 47 chromosomes in each cell, the extra one being a third member of pair #21, so the technical term is Trisomy 21. This dread disorder is a major cause of mental retardation and various physical problems including stunted growth. Its chance of occurrence jumps by leaps and bounds with the increasing age of the mother. Here are the approximate statistics as reported by Apgar and Beck in *Is My Baby All Right?*:

MOTHER'S AGE	RATIO OF BABIES WITH DOWN'S SYNDROME
under 30	one out of 3,000
30–34	one out of 600
35–39	one out of 280
40–44	one out of 80
45 and up	one out of 40

From studies relating mother's age to birth defects, scientists have learned that the possibility of error increases as the aging egg cells wait for the final stages of meiosis, known as the maternal-age effect. There is also a chance of error in the formation of sperm, and a paternal-age effect is known to cause many fresh dominant mutations, particularly achondroplastic dwarfism (see below).

Chromosomal errors sometimes occur in younger mothers when an "overripe" egg is fertilized. The last stage of meiotic division of the egg takes place at fertilization. As the egg travels down the Fallopian tube into the uterus there is some point at which the unfertilized egg becomes "old," is no longer normal and fertile, and disintegrates. Scientists don't know yet just how long after ovulation the ovum is fertile, but they think it's probably less than 24 hours in each monthly cycle. They also think it's possible for an egg to pass its optimal time of conception, become a "bad egg," and still be fertilized. In these cases, an abnormal meiotic division of the chromosomes may have occurred.

Another crucial time of cell division is right after conception. Chromosome abnormalities occurring during the early stages of embryo development can result in a genetic pattern called mosaicism, in which some cells multiply normally and others copy the chromosomal error.

When a fertilized egg has fewer than the normal number of autosomes, 44, it doesn't develop at all. No human tissue, even in miscarried embryos, has been found to contain fewer than 46 chromosomes if the missing thread is an autosome. However, it is possible to survive with only 45 chromosomes if all 44 autosomes are present plus one X (female) chromosome. This pattern, called the XO, occurs in one out of every 2,000–3,000 live births. The medical label is Gonadal Dysgenesis, but let's call it by the more familiar name—Turner's syndrome.

One of the many features of Turner's syndrome is short stature. These girls reach an average adult height of four and a half feet with normal proportions. At birth the first signs are

A girl who is short statured because of Turner's syndrome. (Photo courtesy of Human Growth Foundation)

often puffy hands and feet and excess skin on the neck, which later decreases or disappears. The external genitalia are female, but the reproductive organs never develop. The uterus is very small and the ovaries no more than fibrous streaks. Breasts usually fail to enlarge and menstrual bleeding does not occur. Other symptoms are low-set ears and broad chest with widely spaced nipples. Occasionally Turner's syndrome is accompanied by cardiac and renal abnormalities.

One symptom that usually does *not* occur with Turner's syndrome is mental retardation. This condition should not be confused with Down's syndrome, just because both are caused by chromosomal abnormalities and have similar labels. Children with Down's syndrome (mongoloids) are severely retarded. Girls with Turner's syndrome are not mentally retarded. They often have slight difficulty in visualizing objects in relation to one another, so their non-verbal IQ is often lower than their verbal IQ. As the Human Growth Foundation's new booklet on Turner's syndrome warns, "This difficulty may show up in poor performance in Math, Geometry, sense of direction and manual dexterity." It also notes that mental retardation "has been wrongly claimed in older textbooks."

In fact, sometimes Turner's syndrome is present without any outward signs except short stature. Sexual immaturity at the age of puberty may be the first warning that spurs parents to take their daughter to a doctor. A preliminary diagnosis is easily made by microscopic examination of a few cells from the inner surface of the cheek (buccal smear). Cells are readily identified to be from a female body when they show a dark spot in the nucleus, called the sex chromatin or Barr body. Geneticists concur that this dark spot in normal female cells is the tightly coiled second X chromosome. Even though this X chromosome appears inactive, two X chromosomes are necessary for the full development of female organs. When a cell from a female does not show the sex chromatin, chances are she has XO sex-chromosome pattern and Turner's syndrome. Further chromosome-counting tests on white blood cells can detect conclusively if an X chromosome is entirely or partly missing.

When properly treated with sex hormones, girls with

Turner's syndrome can develop normal sexual characteristics, menstruate, and have sex relations. But they can never conceive children. Ironically, in personality they are usually very feminine, fond of homemaking and child care, and make excellent mothers of adopted children.

Their short stature is due to slow bone development, although growth proceeds at a regular rate each year and bone age is normal to the age of puberty. Human growth hormone has not proved very helpful in treatment, but other growth-promoting hormones can boost the growth rate somewhat. With the right medical and psychological care, every girl with Turner's syndrome can lead a well-adjusted life.

Turner's syndrome is a good example of a short-stature problem that's inherited through an error in genetic makeup even though the parent doesn't have the abnormality. Although this defect is caused by an error in a whole chromosome, other problems caused by defects in dominant single genes can be transmitted to the child even though neither of the parents shows the dominant characteristic. An example of this type of genetic problem is the most common bone disorder, achondroplasia.

A person with achondroplasia has disproportionate short stature, the males averaging 51.8 inches and females 48.6 inches. Although the body size is normal, the head is large and the arms and legs are short in proportion to body length, particularly the upper arms and thighs. Some other symptoms are a prominent forehead, a flat or depressed area at the base of the nose between the eyes, a protruding jaw and crowded teeth. Intelligence is not affected and mental retardation is not a symptom of achondroplasia.

For many centuries all forms of short-limb dwarfism were lumped into one category and considered the same. In recent years scientists have learned that there are over 70 different bone dysplasias, also called chondrodystrophies, that result in short stature, and most are inheritable. Achondroplasia is the best known and most common form. It is one of the oldest birth defects known to mankind, and although scientists have learned a great deal about how it's inherited and how the disturbance of cartilage growth affects the ossification of virtually all of the bones in the body, they don't know how to cure it. In the next chapter I'll deal in greater depth with the physical and psychological problems of these little people.

The mode of inheritance of achondroplasia is through a single dominant gene that is fully penetrant. In other words, you either have achondroplasia or you don't—you can't have just a trace of it. The symptoms are evident at birth. The babies are about average in birth weight but short in length, with small lower bodies in proportion to the upper half. In most cases neither parent has the disease. How can this be if the gene is dominant? Dr. Charles Scott, an expert in this field and currently located at the Texas Medical Center at Houston, explains: "The chance occurrence of a very rare genetic event, a new mutation, is thought to be the cause in over 80% of cases. The majority of affected individuals have average-sized, unaffected parents and siblings as well as a negative family history for dwarfism."

We have already reviewed some of the many possible causes of new mutations in the cells that produce the egg and sperm, but in the case of achondroplasia scientists are pointing more and more fingers at paternal-age effect. Dr. Scott reports, "Statistical studies have shown a significant parental-age effect —sporadic occurrences of achondroplasia tend to occur more frequently when the father's age is greater than 36 years."

Dr. McKusick's note on the subject in *Human Genetics* states, "Paternal age effect is demonstrable in the case of many fresh dominant mutations. If the age of fathers of sporadic cases of achondroplastic dwarfism is averaged, it is found to be 5 to 7 years higher than that of the general population of fathers."

These comments on the advanced age of the father leading to an elevated rate of mutation are echoed over and over in recent literature on genetics, and yet the general public has little knowledge of this danger. As a matter of fact, in the March, 1978 issue of *Good Housekeeping*, the popular psychologist Joyce Brothers was asked if 40-year-old men are too old to be new fathers. Dr. Brothers responded, "Age apparently doesn't affect the quality of male sperm so there really is no physical restriction preventing men from helping to conceive children for many years past their 40th birthday."

Geneticists continue to search for understanding of mutations. Most would agree with Dr. Judith Hall's statement in her "Ask Dr. Judy" column appearing in newsletters for Human Growth Foundation and Little People of America: "We do not really know why mutations occur. We do know some things which make them more likely, like radiation, X-rays, and certain kinds of drugs and illnesses. In addition, we have recently recognized that mutations are slightly more likely to occur in older parents, particularly older fathers. I think it is fair to say, however, that we really do not know why most mutations occur, and we could not tell people to do things differently so that they would not occur."

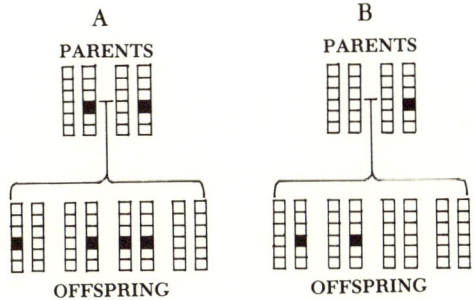

Fig. 17. The dominant gene for achondroplasia is indicated in black in these diagramatic chromosomes. In diagram A, both parents *(top)* have the disorder. Their offspring *(bottom)* have a 25% chance, or one out of four, to inherit the two normal recessive genes *(right)*. There's also a 25% chance of inheriting two dominant genes *(third from left)*. This condition, called double dominant achondroplasia, is usually lethal in early infancy. Most achondroplastics have one dominant and one recessive gene, as shown in the first two offspring. There is a 50% chance of this occurring in the children of achondroplastics. In diagram B only one of the parents carries the dominant gene for a chondroplasia. In this case there is a 50% chance of a child inheriting that gene and being an achondroplastic and 50% chance that a child will inherit two normal genes and not have achondroplasia.

The unaffected parents of achondroplastic dwarfs have the same rare chance of producing a second affected child—that is, another new mutation would have to occur. Likewise, the normal brothers and sisters do not carry the defective gene. The achondroplastic person, however, has a 50-50 chance of transmitting the defective gene and affecting the child (see diagram). If both parents are achondroplastic, there is a 25% chance that it will receive the two normal recessive genes and grow normally; there's a 50% chance that it will receive one dominant gene and one recessive gene and therefore have achondroplasia; and there's a 25% chance it will receive two dominant genes and thus be doubly affected. When the last occurs, the baby doesn't survive more than a few weeks or months.

The genetic pattern of dominant inheritance also occurs in many other types of chondrodystrophies. One is hypochondroplasia, which is marked by generalized bone changes similar to achondroplasia but in less degree. The head and face usually appear normal, but the limbs are slightly disproportionate. Adult height varies between 52 and 58 inches. Dr. Scott believes that this condition is probably rather frequent but that many cases are overlooked as being a result of normal genetic short stature.

More tongue-twisting names label rare bone disorders that are inherited through a recessive gene pattern, with defective genes inherited from both parents. A disorder commonly mistaken for achondroplasia is termed diastrophic dwarfism, but one of the major symptoms that sets it apart is severe club feet.

For physicians to provide adequate genetic counseling, the diagnosis of each specific disorder must be exact. In this regard, and to give you an example of how important correct counseling can be, I'm reminded of a story that geneticist William L. Nyhan tells in this excellent book, *The Heredity Factor.* A newborn boy had tiny limbs and large-looking head. When measured, the head was the right size, but the body was much too small and it seemed that this child was doomed to a growth problem. X-rays indicated an abnormal formation of cartilage at the ends of the growing bones. While the doctors were pondering this, the baby had a visitor, his paternal uncle, who was obviously an achondroplastic dwarf. So the doctors jumped to the conclusion that the baby must have inherited achondroplasia from this uncle.

At that point they called in Dr. Nyhan for consultation. He, of course, knew that a person can't inherit achondroplasia from an uncle via a normal father and mother because transmission requires a parent with the disease or a new mutation.

Dr. Nyhan says, "As a medical geneticist, I looked at the uncle. He definitely had achondroplasia. I looked at the father. He definitely was normal. I looked at the baby. He did look achondroplastic. I seemed to have a problem on my hands. The obvious solution was . . . the uncle was the father."

Aware that a family crisis might be the climax of the story, Dr. Nyhan carefully examined the baby's X-rays. He didn't have achondroplasia. He had a rare and distinctly different disorder called spondyloepiphyseal dysplasia. It too is caused by a dominant gene, but Dr. Nyhan could safely avert the crisis and allay the hospital staff's suspisions by the definite finding that this baby's condition was caused by a new mutation. The child would be short statured, but his adult appearance would be very different from his uncle's.

Genetic counseling can be extremely valuable for anyone who is concerned about transmitting defects. There are several other inherited problems that are accompanied by short stature: vitamin D insensitivity, which we mentioned in the previous chapter; osteogenesis imperfecta, a disease marked by multiple fractures of brittle, fragile bones; and others. Almost any severe birth defect involving major body processes stunts growth.

Ever since the Salk vaccine conquered polio, the March of Dimes has concentrated its efforts on curing birth defects. One of their many services is maintaining a complete file on genetic-counseling centers all over the world. These centers are developing more and more sophisticated techniques for counting and analyzing your chromosomes. They haven't isolated single genes like the one for achondroplasia yet, but they can tell a great deal about your genetic makeup from both laboratory tests and studies of inheritance patterns in your family.

New methods of genetic screening after conception have been developed too. The technique of amniocentesis enables the physician to examine some of the baby's cells that have sloughed off into the amniotic fluid. This fluid is withdrawn through a hollow needle inserted into the mother's abdomen. Down's syndrome, for example, can be detected by this method as early as the fourteenth to sixteenth week of pregnancy. Hurler's syndrome, a bone dysplasia accompanied by mental retardation and other severe problems, can also be detected with this technique. I read the other day about the first selective abortion on a woman bearing twins. Performed in Sweden, the operation removed a fetus with Hurler's syndrome without harming the other.

Screening tests to detect congenital defects, such as hypothyroidism, can also be performed immediately after birth with blood taken from the infant's heel. Many doctors at a recent meeting of the American Association for the Advancement of Science deplored the fact that more physicians don't use these methods to help prevent disabilities.

While I still have you thinking about your genes, imagine this: scientists manipulating genes and chromosomes in the laboratory. Inserting human chromosomes into mice—without killing the cells. Combining a bit of DNA from one organism with a little DNA from another—and creating a new form of life that continues to divide and multiply. Producing a genetically identical twin organism by putting the nucleus of a body cell into the nucleus of an egg from which the nucleus has been removed. Sound like science fiction? No, all of these processes are being done in laboratories right now. The new science is nicknamed genetic engineering, re-forming strands of DNA is called gene splicing or recombinant DNA, and reproducing twin cells is labeled cloning.

These techniques are hot news items in current magazines, newspapers and books. Two I find fascinating are Robert

Cooke's *Improving on Nature* and *Who Should Play God?*, by Ted Howard and Jeremy Rifkin.

Many types of living things from the plant kingdom have been reproduced by cloning, and it has become a valuable tool in agriculture. Scientists are also experimenting with cloning more complicated organisms. For example, years ago in a famous experiment in London, Dr. John Gurdon removed the nucleus from an unfertilized toad's egg and inserted a complete nucleus taken from an intestinal cell of another toad. The DNA code in the nucleus directed the egg to grow into an identical copy of the toad from whose intestines the cell nucleus was scooped. Gurdon thus proved that under the right circumstances the genes in any cell are capable of building the entire organism.

Recombinant DNA techniques involve inserting another gene to change the pattern of growth and heredity. This process often occurs naturally in bacteria and hybrid plants, but now man is doing the controlling. Over the past five years, using a method roughly similar to cutting and pasting, scientists have snipped genes from the DNA of one creature and patched them onto the DNA of another creature. So far the work has been done on a microscopic level, mainly with bacteria. A new bacterium has been made that eats oil and hopefully will be the answer to destructive oil spills. Researchers talk about using gene-splicing techniques to perform feats like helping diabetics produce insulin, figuring out how cells become cancerous, curing birth defects and revolutionizing food production.

The whole field is so revolutionary that scientists themselves called for a moratorium on research for three years while they worked out safety guidelines for what they were doing. Now research proceeds under strict government control, quieting the fears that an untreatable new disease or some dangerous new life-form might escape from the laboratories.

In December of 1977 a group of scientists in California announced that a human hormone had been created in E-coli bacteria. Which hormone? Somatostatin, the growth hormone-inhibiting factor produced by the hypothalamus. The genetic code of the otherwise common bacterium has been altered so that it will manufacture somatostatin, which is completely foreign to its own protein products. Scientists are jubilant over the prospects of producing other hormones by the same means.

Of course the thought of where all this gene splicing could lead is a little unsettling. Take our concern of short stature. Do we want scientists to be able to control a single feature like height? That implies the establishment of an ideal height, and we short people might be an endangered species. After all, can you imagine a tall Mickey Rooney?

7 The Little People

Think big.
　　　　　　　Motto of
　　　　　　　Little People of America, Inc.

In the introduction I mentioned Brian Morris, an achondroplastic dwarf, who said to me, "Comparing you to me is like comparing a man with a broken leg to a man with both legs amputated." I've thought a lot about that remark. What's Brian's world like?

Every time I have trouble reaching something and it annoys me, I'm reminded of the thousands of adults in this country who are shorter than I am. I drive up as close as I can to the automatic bank teller and still have to crawl halfway out the window to reach that darn cylinder. I go to the supermarket. Grocery shopping is one of my least favorite activities for several reasons. The first two most people share with me: everything costs too much, and I hate waiting in line. The other three reasons aren't as common. First, everything I want is always on the top shelf, accessible only to giraffes. Second, inevitably some little kid stares at me, yanks his mother's sleeve and proclaims loudly, "Mommy, there's a midget!" Thirdly, when I unload the groceries from cart to conveyer belt, I can just barely stretch my finger tips to grab the bananas at the bottom of the cart with the edge jammed in my armpit.

Questions: how do Brian and other little people use an automatic bank teller? If they go inside the bank, how do they make themselves seen at the high teller's counter? How do they get the groceries down off the shelves or up out of the cart? And if only one or two children point and snicker at me, how many people gawk at them?

Every annoyance caused by my short height in a world constructed for average-sized people must be magnified many times over for the dwarfs and midgets shorter than me. How do they cope? As I explored answers to this question, I delved into the lives of many little people who cope very successfully. One of the many things I've learned is that reaching things is a minor hole in the road compared to the deep well of social ostracism. Their stories are an inspiration to everyone, short and tall.

Most of the approximately 100,000 severely short-statured people in this country are dwarfs, not midgets. That is, they are disproportionate. We've discussed proportionate short stature caused by hypopituitarism and other endocrine problems, intrauterine growth retardation, malabsorption and other nutritional problems, constitutional delayed growth, psychosocial short stature and Turner's syndrome. There is now hope for children with these problems to grow taller with the right treatment. But for the thousands of little people with bone disorders there is no treatment, no hope at all for growing anywhere close to five feet. So far, injections of HGH don't seem to produce much additional growth, although experimentation on a wide, conclusive basis hasn't been conducted because of the limited supply of the hormone. And being extremely short is only part of the problem, because bone disease also fouls up body proportions.

In the previous chapter I briefly mentioned some of the physical symptoms of achondroplasia, the most common form of over 70 kinds of chondrodystrophy, which means impaired growth of cartilage. Achondroplasia affects about one child in every 40,000 births, including all races and both sexes. The classical signs are present at birth: large head, arms and legs short compared to body length, prominent forehead, flat or depressed area between the eyes. A protruding jaw and poor bite usually results in overcrowding of teeth and dental prob-

A young child with achondroplasia. (Photo courtesy of Human Growth Foundation)

lems. Another common complication in children is ear infections because the tubes leading from the back of the throat to the ears are very short and angled abnormally, so they can easily get clogged or carry infection from the back of the throat to the middle ear.

The legs are almost always bowed to some extent, and if a child's bowleggedness is severe, braces and/or orthopedic surgery sometimes help. Achondroplastics always have spinal problems, usually giving a swayback appearance with curvature of the spine and sometimes a hump. Dr. Judith Hall, a specialist in dwarfism, estimates that 70 percent of all achondroplastics over 18 years of age have problems with pain in their packs and legs. Dr. Charles Scott, another specialist in the field, adds that 50 percent of achondroplastic children under age 10 have trouble with compression of the spine and frequent complaints of pain in the legs, often causing limping. The constriction of the spinal canal pinches nerves and blood vessels. As Dr. Scott describes it, "They may walk for several blocks before they develop numbness, tingling, heavy sensations, weakness, tiredness . . . Rather than admit symptoms for social reasons, the little person may stop to window-shop frequently, or he may stop, stoop and tie his shoe repeatedly." The pain may become so severe that decompressive surgery and bracing are attempted. However, Dr. Scott adds, "By attention to weight control, avoidance of strenuous exercises, avoidance of lifting and shoving of heavy objects, and by maintenance of good muscle tone and strength, many of these individuals avoid serious and radical forms of treatment."

Dr. Scott mentions weight control because obesity is another of the many problems. The combination of little exercise and short stature leads to weight gain that is very obvious. After all, five pounds added to a six foot frame isn't noticeable, but a five-pound increase at four feet is a big jump in weight. (How well I know; at my present weight of 92 I'm a little plump, but as a teenager I weighed in FAT at 100–105.)

The hands of the achondroplastic are short, the fingers stubby, and the feet usually short, broad and flat. The elbows are enlarged, and usually the arms can't be straightened completely. Another sign is loose or "double" jointedness caused by lax ligaments. As Dr. Scott explains in the booklet he prepared for the Human Growth Foundation on achondroplasia, "Many achondroplastic children can flex their finger, wrist and knee joints to an abnormal degree because of ligament weakness. This also contributes to their bowleggedness."

Being short is just one of the many physical problems caused by achondroplasia. Confirming diagnosis is based on X-ray studies of the joints, often the knee, which show shortened bones with ragged-looking ends. As explained in the NIH booklet on "How Children Grow," achondroplasia is a "specific illness in which cartilage formation actually proceeds in an orderly fashion; subsequent bone formation, however, is too slow to keep pace with both the normal development of connective tissue covering the bones and the closing down of the epiphyses." This improper growth affects every bone in the body.

Researchers are trying to establish the cause and cure of chondrodystrophy. So far the greatest strides have been in the area of separating and defining so many different types. They know that an array of enzymatic malfunctions are involved, affecting cartilage and/or bone formation. For years, even centuries, most bone disorders were lumped in the one category of achondroplasia, which led to many misinterpretations of genetic transmission, treatment of symptoms, intelligence level, and life expectancy. Even now many types are mistaken as achondroplasia without careful diagnosis. As noted in the previous chapter, a wrong diagnosis is especially dangerous in predicting the heredity pattern of each disorder.

Achondroplastic children grow slowly. The average male reaches a height of about four feet four inches and the average female a little over four feet. Because of the structural differences, the motor development of the achondroplastic child is slower than "normal" standards. It takes longer to develop the muscular strength to control the large head, so good head control may not occur until the baby is three or four months old. With short arms, the baby may crawl army style on the stomach, or may not crawl at all but instead roll, sit-scoot, or place the head down and pivot the body to get around. Walking begins late, sometimes not until the child is 2 or 3. Ultimately, the achondroplastic achieves all these motor milestones normally.

The biggest problem caused by slow motor development is that so many people equate physical slowness with mental slowness. After all, a three-year-old kid who can't walk must be pretty dumb, right? Wrong! The truth is that the mental development and intelligence levels of dwarfs are not affected biologically by their physical afflictions. Their I.Q. range is the same as the general population's. Most people also equate age with size and assume that a person the size of a young child must also think like a child. We'll refer to this problem again later as it's one of the most difficult stigmas all short people must deal with.

Another frequent misconception concerns life expectancy. Many forms of dwarfism are lethal near birth, and some preclude a long life, but achondroplasia is not one of them. Dr. Scott has reported that true achondroplasia is well tolerated in a newborn and is not often a cause of death. Even so, achondroplastic dwarfs have a hard time finding an insurance company to insure their lives and usually have to pay extra.

All the physical problems rolled into one don't compare to the psychological, emotional and social obstacles that little people must overcome. Not reaching a light switch is not nearly as shattering as not finding a friend or a job. Dwarfs are immediately the victims of social ostracism because their difference is so visible. When average-sized people see a dwarf they react with surprise, curiosity and fear. As one doctor commented, "People are afraid of the unknown. They tend to treat it in a negative way." Social ostracism invades every level of their lives from school teasing to dating difficulties and job discrimination. It causes the terrible loneliness that comes with being different.

John Phillips Strudwick was turned down by 14 girls before

he got a date for his senior prom. John was a fighter born with a form of dwarfism that included two club feet, a cleft palate, a double hernia and a small lung-capacity. Through surgery and his own inventiveness he conquered most of his physical infirmities, but he grew to only 3 feet 8 inches. John never gave up on any goal including getting a date for the prom. "When the 15th one said yes, I couldn't believe it," he said later, "my dating problem is unbelievable."

Featured in many newspaper articles for his achievements in school and the community, John often said, "I can do most of of the things anyone else can. I'm an adult and I want everybody to act like I am." During his college years he served as student-government president and graduated with honors from junior college, and then graduated from Salisbury (Maryland) State College where he majored in psychology. He planned to go on for his master's with a goal of counselor in the vocational rehabilitation field. But first he had to have an operation to relieve pressure on his heart and lungs being caused by curvature of the spine. Complications set in after the surgery, and at age 22 John died.

Dr. Scott sent me a lovely tribute to John composed by his parents after his death, telling about his life in order to inspire other little people. Among his many interests, he was an active member of the Little People of America, Inc. This organization, founded in 1957 by the movie actor Billy Barty, is a powerful force in helping overcome social ostracism. Membership in LPA is limited to persons under 4'10" tall and most of the almost 3,000 members are 2'6" to 4'6", with the majority disproportionate. Whereas the Human Growth Foundation mainly consists of parents of children with growth problems, although anyone is welcome to join, the general membership of LPA is open solely to the severely short statured—the little people, as they call themselves. Average-sized parents of little people can join the Parents' Auxiliary.

Through meetings at local, district and national levels, the LP's share their problems and solutions and get medical advice and current research information from many physicians who serve as their advisors. But most important, they find friends. Every summer hundreds of LP's from the twelve districts get together for a big fling at the national convention. From fashion shows, dances and talent shows to business meetings and panel discussions, these conventions are like those of any group—the cast just looks a little different. They are strongly family oriented, with special activities for the teenagers and the children, the "little littles." Many LP marriages result from friendships blossoming at conventions.

LPA has a Medical Advisory Board, with Dr. Scott as its current chairman, which has a variety of important functions. In addition to providing medical advice, it coordinates research efforts. As Dr. Scott explains, "The LPA is regularly beseeched for membership participation in some researcher's study. There is such a fine line between mutually beneficial studies and offensive inquisitiveness, that selectiveness is a must. Almost yearly someone wants to film a documentary about little people. Most of these film-makers merely wish to make a fast dollar and exploit the members." The Board also advises on the allocation of funds by the LPA Foundation to dwarfism research, vocational training for little people, and placement of Little People for adoption.

LPA has a handbook for members that includes tips on how to handle physical problems like reaching shelves, closet rods, light switches, etc. It has a section on fashion, with suggestions on types of clothing that are most flattering and how to alter a standard pattern. If you have a problem that isn't answered in the handbook, there is bound to be some help from another LP. They have an excellent communications system through newsletters and their well-structured organizational setup, from national officers to the 12 district officers to officers of the many local chapters. But it is very difficult to see the handbook if you are not a member. In all ways LPA is very protective of its own and is very sensitive to situations where its members may be exploited by the "outside." The tips in the handbook are private information for little people only, because needing a stepladder to stir the pot of stew on the stove is a fact of life that should be exposed only to friends who understand. They don't want their everyday problems haggled over and poked at in the marketplace like a strange piece of fish. Who does? It only makes little people feel small. As John Strudwick used to say, forget about "I am big," or "I am little." Instead, "Just say 'I am.' That's good enough."

To join LPA a person first has to be able to say to him/herself, "I am a dwarf and I want to meet other dwarfs." This is a basic step in self-acceptance, which successful little people believe is one key to a happy, well-adjusted, fulfilling life. The other key, they claim, is to recognize the way their size affects people and learn methods of putting them at ease.

How do dwarfs learn to accept their condition? The first step, LPA'ers agree, is to be accepted by their parents. John Strudwick's mother wrote, "From the beginning it was necessary for Nash [John's father] and me to face reality and to plan for the future."

Parents must undergo some deep rethinking. Joan Weiss, a social worker for Johns Hopkins's Moore Clinic, one of the nation's leading dwarfism-research centers, explains, "Parents go through a period of mourning at first for the loss of their perfect child." But, she states in a lovely booklet titled, "My Child is a Dwarf," "Your child's future will depend to a large degree on how you as a parent respond to having a dwarfed child."

Another mother, a nurse, wrote about her feelings when her four-week-old son was diagnosed an achondroplastic dwarf: "The impact of that disclosure can never be related fully. Fear, anxiety, heartache, guilt, depression—all were part of the nightmare . . . Perhaps the most difficult thing I had to accept about Scott's dwarfism is one distressing line I read in a medical textbook under 'Achondroplasia.' It stands out so sharply: 'Treatment. There is no treatment.'"

Apparently one of the major keys to parental acceptance is to not hide the problem in the closet (as some parents do—literally). Joan Weiss comments that it is normal for parents to be afraid that people will reject their child and themselves as well. She advises parents that an answer to insensitive questions such as "What is wrong with your child?" might just be a brief statement that his bones didn't grow as long as other people's. "It is the other person's problem, not yours, if he or she cannot cope with the situation. However, it will be easier for you if you tell your family, friends and neighbors that your child is a dwarf."

The Strudwicks encouraged their friends and John's and their daughter Mary's to visit. "It is very important to take time in the beginning," Pat Strudwick wrote, "to answer all the questions asked—honestly. Why is he so small? Why is his head so large? Why are his legs so short? etc. etc."

If parents deny to themselves and to the child that their dwarfed child is any different, the child will have a much more difficult time understanding himself and finding a satisfying niche in life. Lee Kitchens agrees. Lee, a past president of both LPA and HGF, is a developmental engineer with Texas Instruments and helped design the miniature calculator. He is four feet and one inch tall. He agrees that a matter-of-fact, realistic approach works best for the child, and that often things that hurt the parents don't bother the child. "The parents who are over-protective and deny reality present a major problem. If you can get the parent aside for a short time and let the child react with other children, you'd be surprised. When we see problems in LPA, there are usually problem parents."

LPA tries to discover cases of short-statured children being hidden from society. In an interview with "People" magazine, Kitchens said that parents "live in a fantasy that their child is a slow grower . . . I know of a Long Island lawyer who kept his two kids out of sight until they were 16."

No doubt much of Lee Kitchens's success in life is attributable to his parents' attitude toward him. In a letter advising another mother of a dwarfed child, Lee's mother wrote: "My greatest problem at first was me. I was timid and sensitive to what other people thought and their comments . . . By the time Lee began to be affected by stares and comments, I had built a thick skin and was able to help him . . . I tried to attract all of the neighborhood children to our yard . . . There are always some children, and adults too, who are unable to accept anyone that is different. But I think early exposure to this type of problem helped Lee to form a protective shield."

Many parents and children have trouble accepting the word *dwarf*. It has negative connotations of strange and sometimes evil little men in centuries of folklore and is often used as a term of disrespect and derision. But it is also a medical term and a commonly used one in our language. So wise parents of little people help their children become accustomed to the word in a very positive way. Billy Barty certainly succeeded with his daughter, and I love the story he tells about when she was five years old and playing with some new kids in the neighborhood. She was about 34 inches "tall," and they looked at her and said, "You're an elf." She looked back and said, "No, I'm a dorf." They said, "No, you're an elf." She said, "My Mommy's a dorf, my Daddy's a dorf, and I'm a dorf. You know . . . like Snow White and the Seven Dorfs."

Grace Oliver is another active member of LPA who has learned to accept herself and develop her own capabilities. "I don't consider myself handicapped," she told one reporter, "as everyone in the world is limited in some way. My 'limitations' are just more obvious than other people's." Grace is 34 inches tall, and because her legs are extremely short and weak she depends on a car with hand controls and a custom-made four-wheeled bike to get around. She attends college and hopes eventually to teach the deaf or the blind. She attributes much of her self-satisfaction to LPA. "I've traveled to meetings in Florida, North Carolina, California, Michigan and Oregon. Each time I came back renewed . . . we learned that we are not alone . . . LPA does not withdraw from the average Big World, but we've banded together to learn to cope with it."

Many little people struggle for years to accept themselves without ever seeing another dwarf. Grace Oliver was nine years old before a Shriner took her to a Shrine Circus and introduced her to the clowns, the first other little people she had ever seen. "That's when my whole life more or less turned around."

Brian Morris was 20 years old before he saw another little person. He recently commented to a reporter, "I can't describe . . . it's such a moving thing . . . they crouch down like you crouch down, and they look up at other people like you look up at other people. For the first time, you think, 'that's what I am.' "

Meeting other little people and joining LPA can be an escape from utter isolation. But many little people who have been overprotected from reality or for one reason or another deny the fact of dwarfism don't want to be around other little people because it reminds them of what they are. Lee Kitchens said, "When I meet one I don't know in the street, he may turn and run. When they see me, it's like seeing themselves in a home movie—seeing themselves as they really are." Which can be a shocking confrontation for anyone, short or tall.

LPA tries to help its members adjust to both the "Small World" and the "Big World." Just as some little people find it difficult to adjust to a group of LP's, so some LP's get so dependent on each other that contact with the "outside" is difficult.

Lee Kitchens and Brian Morris are good examples of little people who have adjusted courageously to both worlds. They are well educated and successful in their careers, Lee in engineering and Brian in accounting, and their success depends on their ease of relating with people. Lee, at 4'1", and Brian, at 4'5", both drive cars with adjustable pedal extensions that can be removed and carried in a briefcase on a business trip to attach to rental cars. Lee uses a similar device to pilot his own plane. So does his wife Mary, who is 3'11". Brian and Lee both met their wives through LPA. The Kitchens family in Texas and the Morris family in Michigan live in ordinary suburban homes. The only custom-designed feature is kitchen counters lowered about a foot. They favor low, contemporary furniture. Both couples have adopted children, a boy and a girl each.

The sexual functions of victims of chondrodystrophy are

usually as normal as anyone's except that dwarfed women must deliver by Caesarean section. The problem lies in the genetic risks which vary with the type of dwarfism, as discussed in the previous chapter. There's a 75% chance that two achondroplastic dwarfs will have an affected infant and a 25% chance that the child will not inherit the disorder. As Dr. Scott notes, usually when couples decide not to take the risk they mean that the risk of having a "normal" child is too great and they don't want one. Barbara and Brian Morris decided to take their chances but then endured the agony of losing two babies shortly after birth. The problem was that the babies inherited both defective genes from both parents, and the double-dominant situation is lethal. Subsequently they adopted two "little littles" through the LPA adoption service.

The main goal for most little people is independence, which means a lot more than reaching down the pickles from the top shelf—it means getting a job. The little people who are succeeding in this area are usually the ones who have accepted themselves, understand their own capabilities and make the most of them. Sometimes the physical problems of small size aren't as difficult to overcome as most average-size people think. A four-foot-three-inch plumber tells how people are shocked when they open the door and see him. "They tell me, 'I called a plumber, not a two-foot-two midget.' " With the aid of a stepladder, he says, "I can do anything a normal-sized plumber can, except lift a heavy pipe or a 200-pound bathtub."

Many little people who have accepted their size use it to their advantage in their jobs. Oscar Mayer & Co.'s "Little Oscars" and Squirt Bottling Co.'s "Little Squirt" are examples, as well as little Johnny who became famous calling for Philip Morris cigarettes. Small airplane mechanics can crawl into the wings or other tight places, and small welders can also work in normally inaccessible areas.

Many little people achieve success as entertainers, not only in the honored tradition of clowns but also in serious acting. Billy Barty has made over 110 movies in addition to TV, stage and nightclub appearances. Michael Dunn, now deceased, is remembered for many outstanding movie performances, especially in "Ship of Fools." He said about his dwarfism and his success: "Remember, I was born this way. There was nothing to adjust to. My life has been just like everyone else's—finding out what you can do, what you like to do, and doing it."

Another dwarfed actor currently becoming well-known is Herve Villechaize, who plays the part of Tattoo on ABC's "Fantasy Island," and he teaches Henry Winkler to wrestle in the movie "The One and Only." Says Herve, "I've been acting professionally for 10 years and during that time I've had to refuse many jobs that were offered to merely exploit the fact that I'm a midget. I'm an actor first and it's taken me a long time to establish that."

Many other little people have carved successful careers for themselves, often overcoming great adversity. *Life* magazine ran a feature some years back on Georgia Bowen, a dwarf who after suffering years of abuse and torment, found a place for herself as a foster mother to handicapped children. She took in all kinds of severely physically disabled—paralyzed polio victims, hopeless spastics, cerebral palsy cases, etc., sometimes as many as 12 at once, feeding them, nursing, carrying, tending, loving. The welfare board couldn't believe her success with these children. She explained, "When my kids cry I can go right along with them, for I went through it. I can almost feel myself inside them. I was always in corners. We ought to bring kids out of those corners. That's all I want to do."

When little people are rejected for positions they're frequently told that their small size would prevent them from doing the job properly. I was turned down for a research job with *National Geographic* because I was "too short to reach all the files" and they couldn't be responsible for my "falling off a stool." Little do they know how expert we short people are with stools and ladders!

However, most little people agree that the true reason behind job rejections is that the employer and other workers are uncomfortable around them. As one rehabilitation worker remarked, "Social acceptance is the greatest problem for a little person in getting a job."

Self-acceptance and social acceptance are the two keys to finding a successful, satisfying life. Self-acceptance must come first, because for others to feel comfortable with a little person he must first feel comfortable with himself. Then, instead of waiting for the world to come to him, he must meet the world, at least halfway. As Lee Kitchens phrased it, "You can't expect the world to adjust to you, you have to adjust to it."

When LP's realize that the social barrier between them and the rest of the world is built more of ignorance and curiosity than hostility, it becomes easier to understand and overcome. Mrs. Strudwick wrote, "We taught John to treat the public with compassion and to educate them into the ways of a little person. Never be antagonistic towards an uneducated public. When a problem occurs, attack it, face it immediately."

One method of putting people at ease is to bring the whole touchy subject out in the open. Perhaps asking a potential employer, "Do you think my small size would bother you or your employees?" would open the doors to communication. Familiarity with an issue can destroy ignorance, curiosity and embarrassment and lead to simple acceptance. Did you happen to see the "Phyllis" TV show when Phyllis (Cloris Leachman) entertained a couple who, to her surprise, turned out to be dwarfs? In her funny, bumbling way, she tried desperately to avoid the subject, but her own mistakes kept embarrassing her, such as, "Have some shrimp?" The sensitive comedy showed how everyone became more comfortable when the fact that the dwarfs were dwarfs was no longer a forbidden subject.

A sense of humor always helps any uncomfortable situation, and most LP's enjoy a good joke. Psychologist John Money, who specializes in dwarfism, has pointed out, "Almost without exception achondroplastic persons are endowed with the personality traits of chronic cheerfulness, optimism and confidence."

After repeatedly reading that achondroplastics are often aggressive, I was interested to hear Brian Morris's contradiction.

It's been his experience that most dwarfs are shy and timid, whereas he thinks that average short people are usually aggressive, outgoing, often abrasive. Brian doesn't act shy and timid, however, and he has certainly developed some marvelous techniques in putting other people at ease about his size. He frequently tells the story about the day three black men came up to him. "They said, 'Hey buddy . . . are you in the circus?' I said 'No, I'm not in the circus.' One guy said, 'You're a wrestler then. I saw you down at Coby Hall, right?' I said 'No, I'm not a wrestler.'

"The guy said, 'I saw you on TV then, because I know I've seen your face somewhere before.' I said 'No, you didn't see me on TV.' So the guy said, 'My God, you guys must all look alike.' Then they started to walk off.

"I said, 'Hey you guys, you mind coming back over here for a minute?' I said to the guy, 'Are you a tap dancer?' He laughed and slapped me five and we all parted friends."

It sounds to me like Brian would have fit right in with the sixteen adult dwarfs who underwent extensive psychiatric and psychological testing in a study a couple of years ago at Los Angeles's Harbor General Hospital. The team of doctors concluded that for the most part the little people were happy, contented, well-adjusted people in spite of the obstacles in daily living and the constant taunts of others. One doctor reported, "They have a realistic awareness of what they have to face up to. They were able to recognize that the key thing was the way their size affected people. They were able to develop methods of putting people at ease and making them comfortable." Another noted, "Whenever they walk down the hall they turn heads. You'd think they'd react to that, but they've made a remarkable adjustment. I guess it speaks for the ability of humans to make adjustments to any situation." The study also noted that some credit for the adjustment should go to help from LPA.

Are you surprised, or even disappointed, that this chapter hasn't spouted a pool of information on how the little people cope with their big environment? Well, I could tell you about the woman who's been known to crawl into the frozen-food compartment after a can of orange juice. Or about the man trying to make a phone call: "I holler at someone, 'Put the damn dime in for me.'" This same man, Charles Bedou, a past president of the LPA, also has told about how he copes in the washroom: "I can't use a urinal in a men's room. It's outrageous that I should have to pay a dime, so I crawl under a stall, and I usually go down the line and open them all up."

There are hundreds of physical hindrances that torment those much shorter than me. If you experience any of them, or your child does, I urge you to contact the LPA, and as a member you can find the answers to your questions on how little people cope with their big environment. For the rest of us, even short people like me, let's not concern ourselves so much with how a little person reaches the bank teller's window, but instead be more concerned about how a little person can become the teller. Determined little people find ways to reach counters or turn on light switches by themselves. And the physical accessibility to them of public facilities is being improved greatly by new legislation on behalf of the handicapped. Every change that is made to help those in wheelchairs also helps the little people because their view of the world is from about the same height.

But Brian Morris wasn't talking about reaching light switches when he said he had two legs amputated compared to my broken leg. He was talking about going to school, dating, finding a job, getting married. He was talking about social acceptance.

Tell me, what have you done lately to help a little person think big?

8 Non-Growing Pains

Praise youth and it will prosper.
                    Irish proverb

When I was a child I occasionally woke up in the night with aching legs, probably caused by overexertion. I would tiptoe to my parents' bedroom door and very gently, trying hard not to rattle the knob, open it a tiny crack. Instantly my father was awake. "Katie?" he'd say. "My legs ache," I'd answer. Trying not to waken my mother, we'd both creep back to my bed, where he'd rub and rub my legs, easing away the ache until I fell back asleep. "Growing pains," he'd always say. I thought that was a little strange as I certainly wasn't growing very much, but I never doubted his diagnosis. Just as he predicted, I never had the pains after I stopped growing, and although I was glad to be rid of them I did miss those middle-of-the-night cozy times with my Dad. I realize now that while he was curing my "growing pains," he was also my chief doctor for not growing, a far more painful condition.

Anyone who travels the rough road of childhood and adolescence in a body that's much shorter than average and escapes to adulthood whole, hale and hearty deserves a red ribbon. The blue ribbon and most of the credit usually goes to the short child's parents. Longfellow, as his name implies, probably didn't have much understanding of short people when he penned the regretful line, "Youth comes but once in a lifetime." Most short people would add a "thank God." As one remarked, "I think those teenage years should be outlawed . . . You'd have to pull me kicking and screaming into the past."

Somehow we must all make it through youth and then help our children through the same passage. For parents of short children it certainly helps to be aware of the psychosocial problems involved with short stature, how children might react to them, and how parents can help their children cope with these problems.

Because each family is unique, and each person is unique, any general discussion of psychological problems can't possibly touch on every potential situation, and a solution that works for one may not do at all for another. There are many variables involved with short stature. As Dr. Balaban has noted, "The specific nature of the problems for any specific child will vary depending upon the physical cause of the disability, the possibility of correction, the nature of the family structure, the sex and age of the child, his intellectual capacity and the availability of special opportunities, to name just a few."

But whatever the cause and the specific circumstances surrounding each child's short stature, a few generalities can be made. Every short child faces three realities at one time or another and in varying degrees:

1. He or she is different in a way that is very obvious and can't be hidden.
2. People tend to treat children according to size rather than age.
3. People react to short-statured children by being either insulting, protective or curious.

I listened to a parents' discussion at a Human Growth Foundation meeting recently, and the room crackled with frustration as they tried to cope with problems resulting from these three obstacles. One mother described her daughter's rage at being shoved out of a softball game. Another told about her tiny boy being plopped into a wastebasket at school. Another fumed at the tactless questions strangers ask her daughter about her age and size. Another related how her son had received a concussion from being picked up and dropped in the school playground. A father warned them all of the more serious problems that come with adolescence, especially the heart-rending, embarrassing insults that are waiting in the school locker rooms for small boys with delayed pubertal development. On and on the individual problems pour, all spewing from the basic fact that our society zeros in on the unusual, the different, and the treatment is often not kindly.

It is difficult for everyone, including family, teachers and other children, to treat a small child according to age, not size. Psychologist John Money has studied the problems of short-statured children. "The essence of the problem," he wrote in *Rehabilitation Literature,* "is that all human beings have an automatic unthinking capacity to orient themselves toward other people on the basis of stature and physique as indexes of age and mental maturity. Parents have this problem even when . . . alerted against it. Physicians . . . also are not immune."

Psychiatrists and psychologists have categorized some of the reactions that short-statured children often show when they're aware of their own difference and aware that they are being babied, insulted, protected, and singled out as an object of curiosity:

Denial of reality. Reassuring comments like "I'll grow soon," or "It's not that I'm short—they're tall," might help a child quiet his own fears for a while, but they don't erase the problem, unless the short stature is indeed temporary.

Blame himself or parents. "It's my parents' fault that I'm short" is a common reaction. Blaming others can lead to self-pitying behavior, and blaming himself can lead to self-deriding sarcastic clowning. Every school has its class clowns who gain attention by laughing at themselves, even though they may be crying inside.

Withdrawal. With excessive anxiety and fear of competition and social interaction with the taller age group, these children withdraw into isolation, or prefer the company of adults or younger children. They are probably lonely, unhappy and depressed. When withdrawal leads to chronic depression, the child might use his suffering to manipulate others. By the way, HEW reports that child suicides from severe depression are on the increase.

Regression. Treated like a baby, he agrees to act like a baby, sometimes even regressing to babyhood habits like bed-wetting. When small children are treated at a younger level corresponding to their height rather than their chronological age, they often adjust to the lower achievement level at home or school and may remain dependent on "big people" all their lives. He may feel safe and secure at this more immature level, but then feel threatened if his peers or family expect him to perform at a level consistent with his age and intelligence. The child who has been small but then catches up to his age group is particularly vulnerable to this trap. By performing at a lower level the child has fewer demands put on him and life is much easier—not necesarily happier, but at least it requires less effort.

Bullying. Another response to being treated like a younger child is to resent it and fight against it to prove to the world that although small in size he's big in other ways. But as Dr. Money wrote, "The fight is often ineffectual, for a person of diminutive stature does not have the physical power with which to assert himself in order to be attended to and respected . . . he needs social sophistication and maturity to replace sheer muscle power, but this is the very skill that will be immature." This agressive reaction is the response that earned one boy a concussion. He bullyed and physically challenged the bigger boys in order to feel accepted. Finally, out of sheer frustration of not knowing how to deal with this little gnat buzzing around him, one boy picked the little kid up and dropped him. Some children can carry this response beyond the stage of resentment to fierce hostility. One pediatric endocrinologist says that he has seen several short boys "grow desperate enough because of taunts at school to resort to criminal behavior.

They wind up in the courts in their extreme attempts to prove themselves to their peers."

Extraordinary achievements. A child may try to prove his worth by attempting great intellectual accomplishments or in other independent activities that don't depend on size—music for example. Many small people, from children to adults, seem driven to be absolutely tops in whatever they set out to accomplish, whether it's A's in school, par in golf or president of the Rotary. This compensation for small size can be healthy if it's a goal that's within realms of possibility. I don't think it's particularly advantageous for a five-foot high school sophomore to strive to be a Karim Abdul Jabar. As for myself, I was well into my thirties before I could relax and enjoy belonging to a group without feeling compelled to be chosen president.

Use size to advantage. This reaction can be both healthy and unhealthy to personality development, depending on how the child uses his small size. If he uses it to get out of physical work that he's perfectly capable of doing, it's unhealthy. If he uses his uniqueness as a tool to get his own way and become sort of a tiny dictator, it's unhealthy. However, if a small person realizes, without resentment, that his stature makes him uniquely visible, he can capitalize on this popularity. By letting others know that he expects to be treated according to his age and to his own individuality, he can have a healthy relationship with others and still be the center of attention. Many small youngsters have utilized their size to become cheerleaders, team managers, class presidents, or fill other leading roles in school.

Anyone trying to achieve a goal that depends on the good will of others will be helped by being easily noticed and remembered. But to be willing to stand out in the crowd takes self-confidence, and to handle popularity well takes emotional maturity. My fourth-grade teacher wrote on my report card that being a good leader requires a sense of responsibility and thoughtfulness toward others, and she hoped I could learn to handle it. This remark really stung me and made me very aware of how I was treating others. Everyone in school knew "little Kate," even though I didn't know half of them. I must have acted the queen bee, but that aware, concerned teacher (I can't even remember her name) helped to set me straight (I hope!).

In thinking about the different reactions of small children to how the world treats them, I like the analogy used by one psychiatrist who said, "There are three general types of people —glass dolls that shatter, plastic ones that dent, and tempered-steel ones that 'boing' and rise to the challenge." Of course there are many, many factors that account for the difference. But all psychologists seem to agree that one of the basic ingredients in anyone's feelings and behavior is what psychologists call self-concept, self-image, or identity. How we react to the world depends largely on how we feel about ourselves. And how we feel about ourselves depends a great deal on how the world reacts to us, so it's a rather complex circle. Dr. Balaban gives this simplified example: "A very short child sees himself as being very different from his peers; to him difference may be 'wrong'; he feels he's in some way 'bad'; then he tends to act badly; the response to this bad behavior is negative—someone calls him a 'little stinker'; the notion that smallness and badness are connected becomes reinforced, and the cycle goes on, getting stronger with the passage of time."

Anyone's total self-concept is partly composed of body-image. We are all aware of our bodies and have a mental image of how we think we look, although the image may be unconscious until some change, like an accident, alters it and brings it to our attention. How we think we look has a strong bearing on how we feel about ourselves. Of course height is a very obvious ingredient of body image. Feeling badly about looking short, a feeling that our "bigger is better" society reinforces, can be a very negative force in the development of self-concept. The more the person deviates from the norm in both stature and perhaps also in related physical problems, the more negative the force becomes. A 4'6" disproportionate dwarf exclaimed, "In this society it's okay if you go off the norm, but only if you do it graciously."

A recent study at Yale explored the self-perception and

social interactions of 14 children with hypopituitarism, and five themes recurred in all of them:

1. A feeling of social isolation
2. A sense of powerlessness and vulnerability
3. A sense of incompetence
4. A feeling of low self-esteem
5. Inhibition of aggression

How does a short child develop a positive self-image? How are adverse behavior patterns prevented and positive ones encouraged? Well, parents, I know it sounds like a heavy load, but most psychologists agree that the bulk of the responsibility is yours. For example, Dr. Balaban says that how a "child handles his understanding of his situation is often largely dependent . . . on the kind of relationship which exists between himself and his parents." Joan Weiss writes in her recent study on "Social Development of Dwarfs:" "I have found that the determining factor in the social successes of the dwarfed child is the attitude of the parents towards their child's growth problem."

How do parents help a child build a positive self-image? Here are some of the main suggestions psychologists usually offer:

1. Recognize and accept the child's short stature.
2. Treat the child by age not size.
3. Teach skills in handling the big world, both things and people.
4. Communicate with the child openly and realistically.
5. Give the child the opportunity to fail as well as succeed.

Barbara Taylor tries to combine all five of these guidelines in her treatment of her intrauterine-growth-retarded son Douglas. You will remember that I introduced them in the chapter on human growth hormone, describing that day when, while her three-year-old and her Great Dane threatened our collective peace-of-mind, she shared with me her strong convictions about raising a growth-retarded child.

From the time Doug's growth problem was diagnosed at age two and Dr. Sauls encouraged the Taylors to treat him according to his age and not his size, Barbara has worked at a realistic, honest approach. She believes that "parents can't do enough to help their children realize who they are and what they are . . . they shouldn't play games and hide from the truth. Many short children eventually reach average height, but we knew Douglas would be short, so we've really tried not to give him any pipe dreams. I don't think doctors make parents aware enough of how important it is to be honest with the child and it must start from the very beginning. The child has to know at his level why he's different and why it's happening to him. As the child matures it can be explained more deeply and fully.

"When Douggie was three or four and said he wanted to grow up to be a policeman, I would say—no, you won't be tall enough. It wasn't a putdown because I'd give him alternatives to think about. We used to tease him that he should be an OB-GYN 'cause he'd be right there to catch the baby. Lovingly, we had a sense of humor, no matter how badly we felt.

"You need to be reminded over and over every day every week not to treat a child by his looks but by his chronological age, so you don't overprotect him. There are dangers to being little . . . Douggie got scared when he went to nursery school, so he locked himself in a locker. I became tough on him to learn to do things for himself, like pulling a stool over to turn on a light switch or open a door. The doors at school were very heavy, but a son should open the door for his mother, so I'd just wait while he'd pull and huff and puff, but it really worked. He's learned to cope with any situation, accept any challenge. He's very stubborn and aggressive." [You guessed it—Doug's the boy who ended up with the concussion on the playground!] "But the doctor advised us that he hoped Doug would continue to be aggressive and make friends with a big bully who would help defend him. That's what Doug naturally does—makes friends with the biggest and strongest boys in his class.

"At times he babies himself or blames me—'If you hadn't

had me I wouldn't have to be going through this'—which used to hurt a lot. I've told him that I'm so happy to know him and I can't imagine life without him and I'm not going to accept his blame. I think he's accepted the way I feel and doesn't resent me as much—it's very difficult, because I give him the hormone shots, and they're very painful. It became easier for me when I accepted the fact that I'm not responsible for his being short.

"Everyone has that wart on their nose—it may be hidden but it's there. I tell Douggie that being little is his worst problem and everyone can see it right away and get it over with. Someone else may have a personality problem that takes you weeks to find out about and it's probably much worse than being short.

"It's specially important for him to feel good about himself and how he looks, so I take extra pains with his clothing. He was still wearing an 18-month size when he started kindergarden and all the pants had gripper snaps up the legs and around the crotch, so I had to cut them off and resew the seams."

Doug is a very active, athletic boy. His parents have tried to steer him into sports that don't depend so much on height, like skiing, swimming, gymnastics, or horseback riding, but he prefers competitive team sports. Barb says he wants cheering crowds. Of course his favorite is basketball. Last summer he begged to go away to a basketball camp for a week, which turned out to be an experience that really strained Barb's determination not to be overly protective. When they dropped him off, the first prickling of worry began. Doug was ten years old and less than four feet tall. His roommate was fourteen and the tallest boy in camp. The next night when his parents came back to see a game, Doug was in tears and wanted to go home. A very upset Barb was all for it as she was worried that Doug would get hurt among all those big kids. Her husband sent Barb to the car and talked to Doug privately. No, he hadn't been hurt and didn't feel in any physical danger. The Taylors feel strongly about following commitments, and Doug had committed himself to that camp, so his father decided he should see the week through. The last night, the Taylors returned for the banquet. Amid polite, scattered applause, awards were given out to the best this and the most that. As Barb tells the story, "The last award was announced for 'a boy who wasn't the neatest and he didn't score the most points but he was one of the few who really knew what basketball was all about and he was very special.' When he called Douggie's name the other kids cheered and stamped and roared! The prize was a huge basketball T-shirt that he'll never be able to wear, but he was very proud. So you see, you never know. If it had been up to me I would have brought him home and he would have missed that experience."

Doug Taylor must have used his size to a healthy advantage that week, because his parents have helped him to accept himself and cope in a realistic, positive way with his environment.

Barb struggled for words trying to express her feelings about Doug and his size and finally, her eyes glowing, she bashed down the walls of modesty: "... knowing him ... well, he's just a super kid ... part of Douggie is being short ... he would have been a terrific kid anyway, but this way he's a *super* kid."

But, you say, Doug is an intrauterine-growth-retarded child. He has a problem. My child doesn't have any problems. He's just short. And someday he'll grow.

And I say, are you sure there's no medical problem? If so, then are you also sure there are no psychosocial problems? Have you asked your child?

Most psychologists and psychiatrists agree with Barbara Taylor that the most important facet of helping a child develop a positive self-image is open, honest communication. In many, many cases parents are aware of a child's growth problem long before a doctor makes a diagnosis. In the Yale study, for example, the parents' concern usually began when the children were about age three, but doctors took the common "wait and see" approach, and diagnosis of hypopituitarism wasn't confirmed until about age six.

It's common for both parents and doctors to take a "wait

and see" attitude, which not only can be detrimental to the success of a medical-treatment program but also loses precious time in establishing an open communication pattern. The longer the problem is hidden in the closet, the harder it is to drag it out. When short stature is inherited, short families expect to have short children, and often the subject is never discussed at home, although the children would benefit from frank talk so they would know what to expect from the "outside" world and how to handle it.

At an HGF meeting a very interesting and lively discussion took place after child psychologist Steven Spector's excellent talk, "Helping Parents Cope With Children of Short Stature." One mother volunteered the information that her nine-year-old daughter's growth problem had been confirmed by the doctors when she was six years old. Her question was, when should she discuss it with her child? Dr. Spector, Barb Taylor, and several other parents spontaneously cried in unison: "The sooner the better." The mother, probably overwhelmed by such a strong reaction to her question, defended her failure to discuss the subject with the explanation that she was waiting for her daughter to say something about it. Dr. Spector pointed out, "If you don't ask your children questions, you'll never find the answers . . . don't be afraid of the conversation . . . every short child knows he's short—you won't be revealing anything new."

Often children don't know how to verbalize their feelings or troubles but are relieved when parents find the words for them. Joan Weiss warns that, "Parents often stifle their child's desire to verbalize his sadness by falsely trying to boost his morale, thereby encouraging him to deny or ignore some very real problems. This may cause the (short child) to feel isolated and alone."

As mentioned in the previous chapter, the first step to open communication is for the parents to recognize the fact of their offspring's short stature, accept it and not be offended or repelled by it, and be willing to deal with it. As the well-known pediatrician Lendon H. Smith writes in *Improving Your Child's*

Behavior Chemistry, "Acceptance of the child as he comes in the door is the key to satisfactory child rearing. A child who discovers he is not up to the standards of the particular household in which he finds himself has great difficulty in developing a good self-image."

Parental recognition of the problem seems a simple matter, but studies at Johns Hopkins showed that most parents have a tendency to deny the importance of short stature and the emotional difficulties associated with it. At an HGF symposium, Dr. Sauls commented, "Parents tend to spare the child from talking about the problem by taking him out of earshot when someone asks a question or makes a comment. They are at the same time sparing themselves from facing the problem."

Most parents at HGF meetings agree that if short stature can be recognized at an early age, it is much easier for both child and parent to cope with it than if the growth problem isn't present until late childhood or adolescence. They also agree that it is essential to teach skills in how a short child can handle the big world. Here are a few guidelines I've collected from various sources:

1. Make the physical environment at home as comfortable as possible for your short child. For example, put a lower extension rod in the closet, and low hooks. Have his or her bed out from the wall so short arms don't have to reach all the way across to make it. Keep steady footstools in the bathroom, kitchen, bedroom or other rooms where you expect your child to reach things, and teach him how to use them safely. Make sure there's a mirror that shows the child more than the top of his head. Walk through your child's daily routine and try to see and reach and do everything from his point of reference. Then be aware of his changing abilities as the child gets older, although not much bigger. For example, is the child old enough now to empty the dishwasher if he/she could reach the shelves to put the dishes away? If so, give a lesson on how to do it using a footstool or stepladder.

2. Teach your child how best to cope with the physical environment away from home. At high counters in stores he may

have to find courage to speak up in order to be seen. Most of the hurdles are at school. With the cooperation of the teacher, stools or footrests might be in order for a younger child, but it doesn't take long for children to discard any device that brands them as being different. If the books are too heavy for your child and need to be lugged back and forth, perhaps you could ask the school to allow you to keep an extra set at home.

In helping your child cope with the physical environment both at home and away, do it simply and quickly, without making a big issue of how small the child is and without making him feel guilty that he's causing you extra trouble. When I was young we went to the theater often, and my father always carried along a very thick cushion for me to sit on. I asked him once if it bothered him to carry that big thing every time, and he replied matter-of-factly, "You couldn't see much of the show without it, could you?" That closed the subject.

3. Teach your child some ready answers to teasing and questions about being so little. Here are some comebacks to teasing by other kids:

> "I may be small, but my brain grows just as fast as yours."
> "I was born this way; what's your excuse?"
> "Didn't you know? My mom puts me in the dryer every night."
> Or simply: "God made me small."

Dr. Money suggests that parents help their kids learn how to tease back through a little role-playing at home. He gives the following example:

> Q. "Are you a midget?"
> A. "Is your father a horse?"
> Q. "Why are you so short?"
> A. "For the same reason you were born so stupid."
> Q. "Are you ever going to grow?"
> A. "Are you going to have the tumor cut out of your brain?"

As all of us short people know, teasing doesn't end with childhood. Recently I noticed in the newspaper: "Dear Ann

Landers: I'm a female in my 20's and happen to be five feet nothing . . . I get so tired of people saying 'Gee, you're short' . . . that word 'short' makes me feel inadequate . . . Please come up with a comeback . . ." Ann Landers's reply: "The next time someone says, 'Gee you're short,' reply, 'We're all short on something. You happen to be short on tact.' That should clear a few sinuses."

Children (and adults) are also plagued with rude questions from adults. Trying to maintain the belief that people are just naturally curious and aren't being deliberately insulting and hostile takes a stubborn belief in the basic kindness of humanity. The most prevalent problem for short young children is the "How old are you?" question from curious women waiting in line at the supermarket. I love Doug Taylor's comeback to that one: "How old are you? You tell me first!" Whenever a personal question is asked out of place, a good reply is to ask the same question right back. You can do it with humor and politeness, without being hostile and aggressive, and still get the point across that you are a human being, not a freak, and you expect to be treated like other people.

Many short children are very sensitive to and hurt by the common nicknames: Shrimp, Shortie, Peewee, Peanut, Midget, Stubby, etc. But sometimes these names aren't used derisively but instead as a label to signify being "in" with a group where everyone else has a nickname too—Lefty, Freckles, Stilts, etc. So it may help clear the air for both you and your child to discuss what the kids are calling him and why. Considering my short stockiness topped with red hair, the appellation of Fireplug was rather ingenious, don't you think?

4. Discuss your child's growth pattern and related problems with the teacher. Familiarity always reduces awkwardness, and if each teacher along the way is alerted, maybe problems at school can be prevented. Teachers like cute, little children and often try to overprotect them and make them special pets. Your short child may enjoy this treatment, but it won't help his social relationships with his peers or the development of a positive self-image. Teachers should be reminded not to cre-

ate situations that emphasize size. "Line up according to height," is a real killer. Likewise the teacher who shoves the 3-foot-6-inch boy next to the 5-foot-3-inch girl for a singing performance also shows no sensitivity to the problem. The football coach who told the 5-foot ninth grader to "come back when you grow up" ought to be hung.

Dr. Scott recommends, "Where one or both parents are short, their attendance in class for discussion of short stature usually clears the air of misunderstandings. This is especially useful for children in the first few grades of school." Many disproportionate short-statured parents have found this technique to be particularly helpful. Barbara Morris showed an educational film about little people to all the classes in her son's school.

5. Help your child learn social skills by taking him with you to public places and inviting his friends over frequently. This suggestion is good for any child but is particularly important for one who is trying to cope with being different. To ease a tiny child into the school environment, it might be helpful to take him to nursery school and/or Sunday school first.

Making your home a welcome place for your children's friends will help remove social barriers. Have you seen the show on the Public Broadcasting System called "Feeling Free"? Made by the Workshop on Children's Awareness and sponsored by the U.S. Office of Education, the program features four twelve-year-olds and one fourteen-year-old who, like any kids, play games, sing, tell jokes and have discussions. The big difference is that one is blind, one deaf, one has cerebral palsy, one is dyslexic, and one is a tiny dwarf. The dwarf, Ginny, is a peppy blonde, fun-loving and full of life, just like any twelve-year-old. The film shows her with her average-sized friends at a birthday party, and it's obvious that they are used to her size and so forget about it. Accepted by her friends, Ginny also accepts herself, and doesn't like to refer to her dwarfism as a handicap. "I'm not handicapped. I'm just short." Ginny narrates the segments about her and in the fresh, straightforward voice of youth reveals feelings that we all share. As the camera follows her and a special friend jumping on a trampoline she says, "I'm sort of small and she's sort of large, and we both get teased, so we understand each other. It really helps to have someone who understands."

6. Take extra pains to make sure your short child dresses to appear his or her chronological age rather than height age, even if the clothes must be custom sewn. Appearance is of prime importance in creating the image—for others to judge as well as yourself. A teenage girl should take extra care with hair styles and cosmetics, and if sexual development is delayed, she should be allowed to wear a padded bra if she wishes.

7. Help your child develop skills that allow him to compete regardless of size. Music lessons are excellent. I took piano from first through twelfth grade, and I'm sure that a lot of my self-confidence derived from my success with and love for playing the piano. My teacher insisted that I hit an octave when my hand span was much too small to reach across eight keys, but I kept stretching (with aching pains in my hands to go along with the pains in my legs!) until I forced the little tendons and bones far enough. I must have looked pretty funny perched on the edge of the bench so my foot could reach the pedal, but I never *felt* small because I was so absorbed in the music. So please don't laugh at the smallest boy in the band playing the tuba. Other physical activities for short children: dancing, swimming, running, skating, hockey, skiing, gymnastics, etc. (More on this topic in the next chapter.)

These are just a few of the ways you can help your child cope with being different. By not being overprotective and by teaching skills on how to handle the big world you not only give him the opportunity to be successful and thus build a positive self-image, but you also give him the opportunity to fail. Psychologists warn us that if we don't learn to take little knocks when we're young, the inevitable big knocks that come later will be much harder to handle. As one psychologist described it, "It's far less traumatic to lose your paper route while your parents are still supporting you than it is to be fired from a job that is paying the rent." He went on to say that parents can help children learn from their mistakes by giving the right amount of emotional support. "What is the right amount of support? Enough to keep a son or daughter from being too discouraged to try again, but not so much as to rob them of that precious sting of failure, the great teacher and molder of adults."

All of these suggestions on how parents can help their kids cope with being short depend on an open, trusting, communicative relationship. As childhood advances into the teenage years, the problems intensify, and it's almost impossible for parents to establish open communication at this critical stage if it hasn't been the pattern since babyhood. After twenty-five years of experience as a middle-school teacher, Eric W. Johnson wrote a very interesting book for parents titled, *How To Live Through Junior High School* in which he focuses on the developmental changes from ages ten to fifteen. He points out that the family is still the center of a ten-year-old's world. They look to parents for support and reassurance. In addition, "There is a positive, unsentimental realism about them . . . They are as easy to get along with as they ever have been or will be again for a decade or perhaps ever." So lots of cozy chats about "life" are easiest at this age—about bodies too, including height. The only problem is, height is a very concrete thing and ten-year-olds are concrete thinkers. To counteract the importance of height, parents introduce abstract concepts like personality, intelligence and wit, which are difficult concepts for children to grasp much less to feel are important.

Sometime between ages ten and fifteen begins the "period of turmoil" in which "the direct, probing question from the adult will seldom elicit a cordial response and almost never a revealing one." Johnson describes teenagers' apparent hostility, rejection of authority, the critical examination of themselves and everyone around them, especially their parents, and other of the characteristic hallmarks of this wonderful age that drives parents up the wall. When he discusses adolescents' apparent selfishness and inconsideration of others except themselves and their closed circle of friends, he makes a very worthwhile point: "Self-respect and self-understanding are an essential basis for respecting and understanding others. It is well to see the self-centeredness of adolescence in this light ... There are so many things to understand about one's self that there is little energy and imagination left over for considering others. And this self-examination, especially if sympathetically encouraged, will often lead to a deeper quality of unselfishness and appreciation of others than is possible to the fifth or sixth graders, who may still be unselfish because they have been taught that this is a good way to be."

What are these kids examining about themselves? For one thing, their bodies. Whatever positive body-image they've been able to establish up to this point in their lives may get tossed out the window and the mirror along with it if it doesn't match up to their suddenly idealistic, perfectionistic view of themselves. Now the struggle for a self-concept is engaged in earnest. Childhood was just a preliminary skirmish leading up to the big Q: "Who am I?"

Erik Erikson, the noted scholar of adolescence, describes a sense of identity as "a feeling of being at home in one's body." But what if that body is short? Even worse, what if that body is short and childish? So often short children develop slowly. How can a fifteen-year-old boy feel "at home in one's body" if the body's a head shorter than his friend's and he's afraid to reveal his undeveloped private parts to the guys in the locker room shower?

All of us parents with teenagers know that for a boy, being tall is "cool" and being short is "weird." For a girl being tall or short is "wierd." This all-consuming drive for conformity can unleash the calmest mother's wildest emotions. And you should see what it does to me when my fifteen-year-old daughter refuses to carry an umbrella or even wear a hat or scarf in torrential rains because "no one else does."

What handy little tips do I have to tell parents specifically on how to help teenagers cope with being short? Here are a few offerings:

1. You can reassure him or her that delayed sexual development means continued growth. Sexual maturity signals finality to longitudinal bone growth, so the longer that process is delayed the more chance the child has of increasing height. If you were a late developer, let your child know, so he or she can find some comfort in seeing that it's possible to end up looking like a "regular person." Of course these reassurances probably won't show much by way of obvious results in the behavior of kids who want to be taller *now,* but maybe a little comfort creeps inside somewhere to bolster a drooping ego.

It's important for parents to understand that it's very difficult to get children to cross emotional bridges that may be appropriate for their age but not for their physical appearance. Until a teenager reaches certain phases of pubertal development he or she may be temporarily more comfortable with younger friends who are on the same emotional level. The delayed release of sex hormones affects the emotions as well as physical appearance. Testosterone gives the male a tremendous sense of power and confidence. A girl becomes more emotionally secure as estrogen changes the contours of her body so that she looks like her friends.

At one time a child may be at different ages chronologically, sexually, biologically, intellectually and emotionally. In such a confusing situation, the child should be allowed relationships with whichever age group he feels comfortable in, providing there is plenty of opportunity for continued emotional growth until he can fit in with his peers.

2. The biggest advantage of being short is being different, but don't tell your immature teenager unless you want a retort like: "You don't understand—I don't want to be different." Maybe she liked being different and teacher's pet at age eight, but not any more. Wanting to be different, to stand out from the crowd, is a sign of maturity at any age.

3. Reassure yourself that any effort you made when your child was younger to give him a realistic attitude to his growth pattern will pay off in the long run. Also reassure yourself by reading all you can about adolescence so you will know that it's

not all your fault and you're not required to solve all your child's problems. Have you read Margaret Mead's *Coming of Age In Samoa?* This wonderfully wise woman studies and writes about humanity with loving, piercing insights. By describing what she observed in Samoa, she shows how our contrasting social environment influences our children's development. It's a classic, you know, and a very readable one.

4. Continue to provide emotional support, even if it's unasked for or denied when it's given. Words can hurt far more than sticks or stones, as we all know, and negative remarks at home cut deeply and often wound forever. As one family counselor, Dr. Honor Whitney at Texas Women's University explained, "Many parents thoughtlessly contribute to the misery teenagers feel over their physical development. Parents 'kid' their children with nicknames like Runt and Fatso, and the words give the youngsters a self-image they come to accept." Dr. Whitney's studies on how to give and get emotional support was reported by Norman Lobsenz in *Woman's Day* magazine recently. She found that most people vividly remember the putdowns parents dish out. "Most of us are simply unaware of how negative our words are," she believes. One of her many guidelines in developing the habit of giving emotional support is to "learn how to detect the signs that indicate when another person wants or needs your support but does not know how or is unable to ask for it." Then . . . "Develop the habit of making a positive statement." In other words, watch out for the "Hey, Shrimp" blues and try to reinforce a positive body-image.

5. Do as pediatric endocrinologist Virginia Weldon of St. Louis Children's Hospital does: "I tell a boy to go out and next time he's in a supermarket or shopping center to look around him and see what variety of shapes and sizes of people—normal people—there are walking around the street and to see if he has to look exactly like his peers to be a successful adult."

6. If your adolescent is severely disturbed by a lack of height, seek professional help. Short stature is a medical and/or a psychosocial problem, and your pediatrician can steer you to

a pediatric endocrinologist and/or a child psychologist for help. "Most of the things we endocrinologists deal with," *Medical World News* quotes Dr. Judson J. WanWyk, who heads the pediatric endocrinology clinic at the University of North Carolina Hospital, "are body-image disorders. I have sympathy for people with demonstrable pain that's directly attributable to distortion of their body image." As I mentioned in chapter three, hormone therapies can help some teenagers who are suffering psychologically from delayed adolescence.

Most teenagers feel that parents can't share this self-examination and identity-seeking process. I asked my short 15- and 18-year-old daughters, both very bright and usually communicative with their mother, what a parent can do to help a teenager cope with the problems of being short, and they both replied, "Nothing." But I think that's because they're still in the grip of those years, and they can't see the forest for the trees. So I asked my 21-year-old niece, Harriet Muth, a recent escapee from teenagism (I hesitate to say she's through with adolescence as I'm not sure any of us ever escape that phase completely!).

Harriet's growth pattern is called constitutional delayed growth with delayed adolescence, which affects far more boys than girls, although doctors are now realizing that many more girls are affected than once thought. I asked Harriet to write me about her "short" experiences, and I think her story is very interesting and inspiring. Harriet now is about 5'4" and 115 pounds. She remembers being 4'9" and 75 pounds in *10th* grade, and had been short and skinny all of her life. She says:

"Actually, it wasn't really so hard growing up short as it was growing up skinny . . . The worst was having skinny legs and no chest. In seventh grade, about the time when 'normal' chest development becomes noticeable, there was a doll on the market called a 'Flatsy' doll. The TV jingle to advertise it went: 'Flatsies, Flatsies, they're flat, that's that.' Well, I received a note in science class saying, 'Muthies, Muthies, they're flat, that's that.' That really stung, although I'm sure the other girls weren't exactly overflowing... Another event I remember was being sick and friends bringing me my 'first bra' as a get well present. I guess the possibilities alone were suggestive enough to make me feel better."

Harriet remembers that being small made her extremely shy, but also... "I think it developed a tough core. After a while you can laugh at anything." When she started high school she was determined "to bring out the core 'tough' and put away the 'shy'. Being outgoing gives a definite boost to physical smallness. 'A little loud and a little proud' was the answer to being totally overlooked.

"Another thing that helped was the fact that I was pretty strong for my size. I still hold the high school record for flexed arm hang in gym class, and a lot of people called me 'muscles.'

"I also did crazy things like backpacking—in the winter too. I think I had to be a little different, maybe a little bizarre, to gain some recognition. If you're small plus the same as everyone else, you blend into the woodwork very easily."

Harriet's growth-spurt began in the 11th grade, and she shot up almost six inches in two years. Here's how she traces her adolescent development:

10th grade—4'9" tall, approx. 75 lbs.
12th grade—5'2–3" tall, 95 lbs.
Menstruation—middle of 12th grade. ("That never really bothered me.")
Freshman year college and summer before—most sexual development.

"First three months of freshman year I gained 20 lbs. and started looking like a human being instead of a human bean! Didn't need to shave under my arms until sophomore year and just finishing developing my chest this (junior) year. I've stopped growing I think at 5'4", 115 lbs."

In answer to my question about how parents can help kids cope, she replied, "As far as giving advice goes, I think that's impossible. 'Don't worry, you'll grow out of it' doesn't help the current situation, and peers can be quite dreadful about the whole thing. You just have to live through it, and then look back on it."

Then Harriet hit the nail on the head: "I think the best thing my parents ever did was to encourage me to go out and tackle the world even if it was a little bigger than me . . . That's the only advice available." The only . . . and the best, don't you think?

You see, we keep coming back to the same words: encourage . . . support . . . praise . . . acceptance . . . love . . . to help any child, any age, cope with any problem.

Helping your short-statured child doesn't involve any special new techniques in child rearing, just a few special refinements and areas of awareness. Every parent owes every child a comfortable feeling about their bodies. Sometimes we get off the track and think we owe them ice skates or chauffeur service or a college education. But the things and services we provide for them are extra and not obligatory. Our basic debt is simply a feeling of personal value.

My father's instant response to my needs in the middle of the night was typical of his constant support, his striving to help me grow in every way, not just up. Because he believed in my intrinsic worth, whether I was short, tall, or had two heads, I grew to believe in myself, and finally the pains went away.

9 I Like Being Short

> *You can't tell the depth of the well
> by the size of the handle on the pump.*
> Anon.

Let's load one side of a big, old-fashioned scale with all the disadvantages of being short and pile up the advantages on the other side and see what we've got. First, concentrate on the little (pardon the expression) everyday things that can annoy short people, the physical things that are a constant reminder that the world was not constructed for the small. We all have our grudges, so I'll list mine and leave room for you to add yours.

Things That Bug Me Because I'm Short

1. Crowds
2. Shopping for clothes and shoes
3. Driving cars
4. Kitchens (reaching shelves, cleaning the top of the refrigerator, etc.)
5. Dangling feet
6. Supermarket high shelves and deep bins
7. Pharmacists' high counters
8. Airlines' high counters
9. Fast-food restaurants' high counters
10. All other high counters everywhere
11. Drinking fountains

12. Pay phones
13. Adjusting a high shower head
14. Hangers in motels that you can't remove from the rod
15. Reaching motorist-aid phones
16. Reaching the cylinder at automatic bank depositories
17. Speaking at lecterns or standing microphones
18. Mirrors too high to see in
19.
20.
21.

Most of these physical disadvantages have to do with reaching. I try to remind myself of the great exercise I'm getting and that maybe all the stretching will help me to keep from shrinking. I also am no longer too timid or self-conscious to say, "Excuse me, but could you please reach down a can of peas for me?" Many aids are available for the home: revolving turntables for kitchen and closet shelves, continuous cords to the floor for window drapes and blinds, shower-head extensions, closet rods that hang down from the top rods, plus all sizes of sturdy footstools and stepladders, some very attractive that add to a room's decor.

Fortunately for us little people, new laws meant primarily to help the physically handicapped in wheelchairs are bringing things like drinking fountains and pay telephones within our reach too. Even the problem of climbing that big step into a bus must eventually be solved by all public-transportation systems.

For twenty years I drove a car with a pillow under me, a pillow behind me, and an aching leg that barely reached my toes to the gas pedal. Then six years ago I bought a Buick with an adjustable steering wheel that I can lower almost to my lap, and I had the track of the whole front seat moved up and the back tilted forward a little. Presto chango—pure driving comfort! I have over 75,000 miles on it and I'm reluctant ever to give it up. Of course, no one over five feet can fit in the front seat when I'm driving! By the way, most people think that little

I Like Being Short 185

Following are some photos of me showing advantages, disadvantages and compensations of being 4'9". They were taken by Linda Jewell.

Kitchen cabinets can be a real struggle.

Sometimes I need an extra lift to help stir the stew.

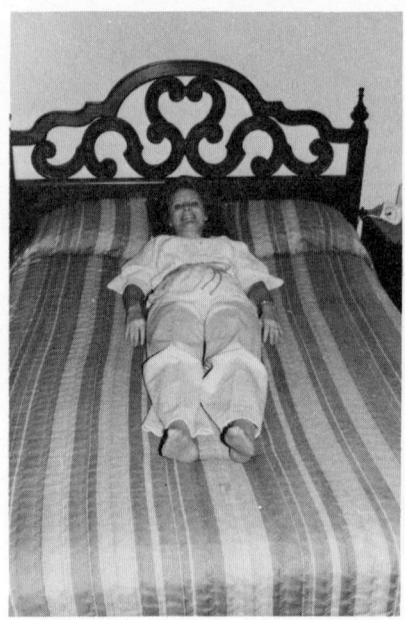

I have lots of room in a regular-sized double bed.

Everyone should have a comfortable chair that fits their height.

My dining table was cut down to suit me, but people of average size don't notice the difference.

I Like Being Short   187

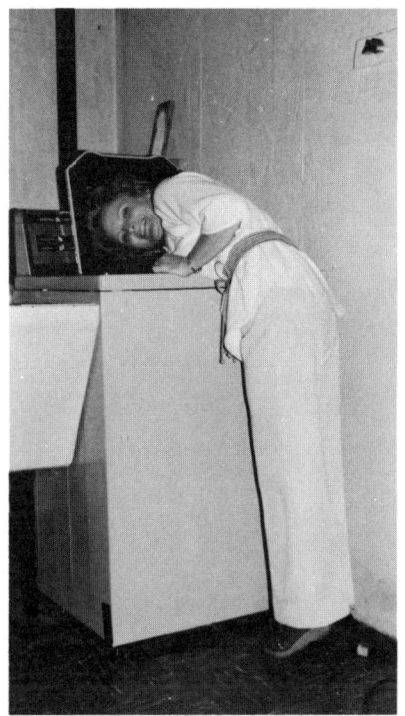

I had the seat of my car specially adjusted for my height.

I should have brought my stool down to the basement to help me reach the laundry out of the bottom of the washing machine.

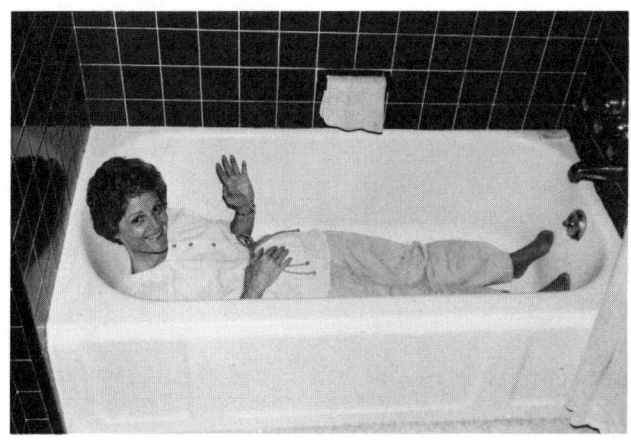

I can stretch out comfortably in a bathtub.

cars are made for little people. Wrong! Several years ago I went to the automobile show at McCormick Place in Chicago and I sat behind every steering wheel, from Jaguars and Rolls Royces and Cadillacs to VW's, Fords and Chevrolets. I tried sports cars, sedans, little ones, big ones. Result of my survey: the bigger the car the better I could see over the steering wheel and reach the accelerator at the same time. First prize went to every big, luxurious model that had the 4-way power seat. No matter how short you are you can drive a car these days, even if you have to add pedal extensions or hand controls.

Another problem for short people that's becoming easier to solve is finding clothes, stylish clothes, that fit. For years small women have shopped in the preteen and junior departments, making do with fashions geared and cut for children and teenagers. In 1977 Matthew Love Fashions of New York started a new, very successful size-category: clothes for the petite miss. They're geared for mature women between 4'10" and 5'3" and under 115 pounds, and the sizes are labeled petite 4 through 12. At first buyers at department stores hesitated to stock the new item even though market research indicated a customer pool of 14 million. As soon as short women heard the news the stores began to be attacked by a small army! Now at least ten other designer lines have joined the bandwagon, and finally I can buy a dress. What a delight to slip a fashionable creation on and have it feel made for me—and with a moderate price tag. For your information, my 4'9"-92-pound figure, with "vital" statistics about 34-24-33, fits perfectly into a petite 4 with no alterations needed, not even hemming. That, my friends, is *luxury!*

Other short women always ask where I buy shoes: my best source for stylish 3½ B's is Naturalizers. Sometimes I search the children's department for casual shoes, and a few mail-order houses specializing in hard-to-find sizes advertise in the back of women's magazines like *Woman's Day* and *Family Circle.* Fortunately, many children's styles look very adult these days, although it's hard to find a high heel. By the way, remember to keep all your clothes proportioned to your body, including shoes. Very high heels may add to height, but they can also subtract from poise and look silly on a very small woman.

For panty hose, try J.C. Penney's. Their "short" size is the only short on the market that's short enough for me. Interestingly, very tall women say that Penney's is the only place to find long enough panty hose too.

Another innovation in clothes that is helping my wardrobe tremendously is "Stretch and Sew." If you like to sew at all, I highly recommend this easy method of tailoring clothes to fit *you*, no matter what your size or proportions. I took the eight-lesson introductory course that's offered at all Stretch and Sew stores throughout the country and learned to adjust patterns for me. Now I use the same ones over and over for slacks, suit jackets, skirts, etc. Believe me, I'm no wizard at the sewing machine, but this method is easy and very satisfying as I always end up with a garment that fits. And it's definitely an advantage to be small when it comes to buying fabric for clothes.

Stretch and Sew has patterns for men too, and every short male who has a woman to sew for him is very fortunate because short men have it much rougher in shopping for clothes than short women. Ten years ago, men's average shirt neck was 14½ to 15, but now it's 15½ to 16½. A man wrote into my local newspaper looking for a size 14–31 shirt, and was answered that only Arrow Shirts in New York still make them that small, only in basic white, and they have to be special-ordered.

There are a very few men's stores that specialize in short men's clothing. One of the most complete is Napoleon's Closet, which has three branches in the Detroit area. Manager Rick Barker, who at 5'7" thinks he's short, showed me his complete line from sports wear and suits to top coats and accessories that are geared for men 4'11" to 5'8". They carry 14½–31 shirts, size 5 shoes, and size 7 gloves. If you're smaller than that, I guess custom-made clothing is the only answer. It's expensive but long-wearing, and at least you have the satisfaction of knowing you look your best. It's better to have one really sharp suit than three that look better on the hanger.

Let's see, what other disadvantages can we minimize? Well, it's hard to eliminate the dangling-feet problem, except at home. There of course you should picket for your right to have at least one chair that's comfortable for you, no matter how small or low to the floor it needs to be. After all, Father has had "his chair" for generations, and now it's time for equal rights for everyone else in the family no matter what age or size, just like The Three Bears. Anywhere out in public the chair will probably be too high, and we're stuck with pinched circulation and loss of dignity. In school, I always bee-lined for the chairs with rungs; in restaurants I opt for the straight, hard chairs versus the deep, cushy benches. I often sit on the edge of my seat, but not out of suspense, and I tuck my legs up under me whenever possible, especially in the movies ever since I became too old to prop them up on the seat in front of me when the usher wasn't looking.

As for feeling claustrophobic in crowds, crushed between belts, butts, and bellybuttons, looking down at everyone's feet makes me slightly less uncomfortable than up at heads. It also protects my face from wandering elbows, and I'm not adverse to doing a little elbowing of my own if the crowd is rude as well as crushing. But the air is always bad down there, so avoid it if possible by arriving early to the football game, theater or whatever, and leaving late.

As annoying and inconvenient as these types of disadvantages of short height may be, they are still just *physical.* Most of these problems are caused by the obvious fact that we're a lot smaller than average, and industrial designers build things relative to the size of Mr. and Mrs. Average. Since World War II an exact science called anthropometry has developed which compiles data on human dimensions specifically to aid industrial designers in fitting the size of a product to the size of the user—things like stadium seats and telephone touch-buttons. I read that public telephones were positioned so 95 percent of the population could reach them, which sounds just dandy, except that the 5 percent who can't reach equals 12.5 million people. But still, these problems are only a matter of physical

I Like Being Short

adjustments, and with ingenuity and gumption they can usually be overcome. It's the psychological disadvantages that can cause the real hangups. But before we add them to our list, let's turn the other cheek and consider a few physical advantages to short stature. Once again I'll list a few ideas I've collected, and you can add your own:

1. Little hands for doing needlework or other intricate tasks
2. Fitting into back seats of two-door cars
3. Lying down in bathtubs
4. Stretching out on regular-size beds
5. Sitting comfortably in airplane coach seats
6. Wearing snazzy hats in snazzy sports cars without hitting the roof
7. Fitting into crowded elevators (that can be both good and bad!)
8. Fitting into children's sizes—they're cheaper
9. Other people can see over you in the movies and theater and at football games, etc.
10. Hide easier
11. Get out of a lot of work bigger people are expected to do
12. Pack more clothes in a suitcase
13. Crawl into attics and other small places
14. Getting into the movies for half price long after age 12
15. As one bumper sticker says: "Short people are better lovers."
16.
17.
18.

A word about that last item: After all, short people are cuddly. Our bodies are usually agile, coordinated, easily maneuverable, and there's a lot of room in bed. Small women have it made as most men of all sizes like to be physically bigger than their women. Small men often question the demand for their sexual prowess, but evidently women of all sizes enjoy the capabilities of small lovers. They can't physically impress power over their partners, so instead they are tender, loving, and creative—just what all women are looking for. Have you ever noticed that most jockeys marry very tall women?

There are really lots of things small bodies can fit into more comfortably than average-sized people. Personally, I would rather fit comfortably in an airplane than reach the top shelves at the supermarket, wouldn't you?

Whether the physical pros and cons balance each other out depends on your degree of short stature and your ability to, as Bing Crosby sang, "Accentuate the positive and eliminate the negative." Ask yourself: (1) What are the physical things in life that really bother me and/or my short family and am I doing all I can to deal with them as easily as possible? and (2) Am I taking full advantage of all the good ways I and/or my short family fit into our physical environment?

I can hear someone out there yelling—"Sports! What about sports? I'm too small for sports!" Okay, let's load sports onto our scale next. We'll put all the sports that usually require you to be tall and fairly big to compete successfully on one side, and the sports in which body-size really doesn't matter on the other.

All sports require strength, but a tall body isn't automatically strong and a short body isn't necessarily weak. The National Athletic Health Institute compared the physical attributes of many top athletes from various sports—football, baseball, tennis, etc. Who scored the highest in the battery of conditioning tests? Bill Shoemaker, the winningest jockey of all time, scoring over 7,000 victories in 30 years of racing. Said Dr. Robert Kerlan, "Jockeys as a group have the best over-all conditioning of all athletes. We were surprised with the jockeys' cardiovascular endurance, their upper and lower body strength and their flexibility . . . Billy Shoemaker is in better physical shape than many of the Los Angeles Rams." The Shoe is 47 years old. He stands about 4'10" and can weigh in at 103 pounds including his saddle.

Sports for Talls and/or Bigs	Sports for Shorts and Others
Basketball	Golf
Football	Skiing—Snow and Water
Baseball	Skating—Ice and Roller
Discus and Javelin Throwing	Hockey—Ice and Field
High and Broad Jumping	Sledding
Running Races, especially hurdles & sprints	Squash
	Racquetball
Boxing, except lightweight	Handball
Wrestling, except lightweight	Horseback Riding, esp. racing
Weight Lifting	Soccer
	Tennis
	Car Racing
	Skateboarding
	Bowling
	Gymnastics
	Swimming, esp. synchronized
	Diving
	Fishing
	Jogging
	Long-distance running
	Pole vaulting
	Cycling
	Boating
	Archery
	Riflery
	Hunting
	Fencing

Still think there are no sports for short people? The trouble is that the big three—football, basketball, and baseball—are the great All-American pastimes emphasized in our society at all age-levels, from little-league to professional. At many schools it's hard to find any other sports to participate in, and many teenage boys suffer painfully if they can't compete in one of these three. Track, soccer, tennis and swimming are becoming more popular in schools with the proper facilities, and short kids have a better chance in these sports. One handsome, 5'2" high school senior explained to me that he has specialized in diving because, "A short person looks like they're bouncing higher in the air off the board, and I have more room to do stunts before I enter the water." My 5-foot daughter likes synchronized swimming and is glad she doesn't have a "bigger body to lug through the water."

Little Doug Taylor is a walking encyclopedia on sports, and he knows who the shortest professionals were in the big three during 1977:

Baseball: Fred Patek, 5'4" shortstop for Kansas City Royals
Basketball: Calvin Murphy, 5'9", Houston Rockets
Football: Howard Stevens, 5'5", 162 lbs., Baltimore Colts

In December of '77, *Time* magazine featured short men in professional football: "Dashing to touchdowns, leaping to bat down passes or darting past befuddled defenders for a crucial reception, the runts have provided some of the most thrilling moments . . ." The success of the 5'5" to 5'10" running backs in college and professional football has been good news to the 5-foot high-school running backs, who now at least get the opportunity to play a little. Of course the small guys have to play five times better than the big guys. As Howard Stevens said, "The important thing is to get the chance to show what you can do and not get written off on size alone. Then you've got to cash in on that chance, because as a small man, you may not get another."

Now we're creeping from the physical arena to the psychological, and here the disadvantages to short stature get a whole lot heavier. Add this one to the scale:

Social Prejudice

As we discovered in the first chapter, social prejudice is a hefty load, encompassing lack of respect, discrimination in jobs, segregation in school, underestimation of intelligence and other abilities, weak image in the business and professional world, and on and on.

Are there any psychological advantages to short stature that help balance our scale again? Well, try these:

1. Character-builder
2. Friend-maker
3. Motivator

These words have a nice ring to them, don't they? I wish I'd been the first to list them in this context, but I'm not. They belong to David Hornstein, an attorney in Washington, D.C.

Every new member to the Human Growth Foundation receives a membership kit containing an abundance of marvelous information about growth. One of the items is a copy of a letter written by David Hornstein to "a 16 year old girl of severe short stature," telling her about how he managed to find a successful, fulfilling life in spite of, or perhaps because of, the fact that he's 4'7". He summarizes all of his observations in these three concepts: character-builder, friend-maker, motivator. They carry a lot of weight, don't they?

Building character means knowing and liking yourself, overcoming your deficiencies and enhancing your strengths. Like all short kids, David Hornstein had his turn being rejected and teased, and he had to face up to his own body-image, realise how it affected others and react in a way that wouldn't lead to further rejection. Hornstein wrote, "I didn't get sore. I didn't become cynical. I didn't get smart alecky. And I didn't become a cry-baby. I just went on being nicer than the rest of them. Patience and confidence that I was as good as they brought me back into the gang."

When you're young, small and the brunt of negative attention, you're forced to learn to roll with the punches, both physically and mentally. Maybe this results in faster reflexes in both areas. It also opens doors to hidden recesses of the human character that average-sized people without physical deviations never realize they possess. Adversity breeds strength.

Short people have to work at earning respect, but they also get what Hornstein calls the "underdog break." Because less ability is expected from a short person, a performance that's acceptable for average-sized people is considered extraordinary for a short person, and these standards are applied to all fields of endeavor, mental as well as physical. Hornstein discovered this break and made it work in his favor when he began practicing law: "In Court the Judge and the juries expected less from me than they did from my bigger and more imposing adversaries . . . All I had to do was display average intelligence and average ability and right away they gave me credit for more than I deserved."

Wrestling with the questions "who am I?" and "what am I?" usually is an especially painful experience to anyone with an obvious physical deviation like short stature. But being forced to look deeper into oneself can mold self-respect and integrity. And being forced to overcome other people's prejudice toward you can build determination and a gritty desire to excel.

David Hornstein commented that short stature "will give you a keen appreciation of the real values of life . . . you will not be upset by trivia. You will find true contentment when you unlock the secret of counting your blessings."

Not only does being short force sharp perspective on some of life's major problems, but it also makes a person sensitive to little things. I find that I am particularly drawn to the tiny, exquisitely perfect shells on the beach, while big people hunt down big shells. Beyond noticing small things in nature, I think small people are more sensitive also to slight nuances of feeling and thought in themselves and others, which leads to deeper understanding and awareness.

One of the many ways in which being short makes friends

is that a short person is noticed and remembered. Of course standing out in a crowd is the last thing most teenagers want, but eventually adults recognize the value of appearing unique and strive to be noticed. When I switched from an environment where everyone at school had known me for years to college, where there were thousands of new, anonymous faces, I quickly learned for the first time the tremendous advantage of instant notoriety. Everyone knew who I was the first week.

Of course being noticed and remembered doesn't mean being liked, but short people have another asset going for them—it often makes others feel protective. Taking advantage of this reaction and playing the weakling won't win friends in the long run, but the protective instinct towards smaller people is a friendly one and can be a good opening to a friendship. Sometimes big people have an aura of threatening power that leads others to be wary or distrustful, but small people don't have that problem.

It is our apparent weaknesses that others identify with, not our strengths, and the obvious weakness of short stature draws people's interest. My husband often repeats that it's important to have others overestimate your weaknesses and underestimate your strengths. That's easy for short people because that's how society reacts to us automatically.

The kind of person who shows self-respect, integrity and sensitivity towards others is the kind of person who makes friends. A short person who has accepted his own body-image strives to make others comfortable with it also. David Hornstein works at showing plainly that he's not sensitive about his looks. He says that when he does public speaking he often relaxes the audience by starting with, "The only reason I'm here tonight is because they wanted a short speaker."

Now that I think about it, I realize that all my life most of my best friends have been quite tall. But being small is certainly a friend-maker with other short people; it's like an invitation to an exclusive club. Even those too tall to join Little People of America feel a special camaraderie, that unspoken "you know what it's like too" feeling that ties people together.

My niece Harriet commented, "It gives me a little bit of pride (I don't know why) to have a history of short people in the family."

The forces that build character and make friends also motivate a person towards a successful life. A strong character in a short body that stands out in a crowd just naturally wants to do well. I know a young 5'1" woman who is struggling in New York trying to establish a career as a dancer. She says that most tryout announcements for chorus girls specify for over 5'4" only. Her reaction: "I'm too small for the chorus, so I'll have to be leading lady." I don't think it's entered her mind to give up.

Being a short male in the American business world must be a real motivator these days as that's where prejudice seems to lurk most dangerously. Without height and bulk to impress a client or customer or boss, the short businessperson must display tall amounts of hard work, intelligence and personality to balance his shortcomings (sorry—couldn't resist).

Short people in the entertainment world seem to fare much easier. Many, many famous actors and actresses, singers, comedians, directors, and producers are quite short: Al Pacino, Charlie Chaplin, Joel Grey, Peter Lorre, Edward G. Robinson, Jimmy Cagney, Dustin Hoffman, Paul Simon, Sammy Davis Jr., Paul Williams, Nancy Walker, Paul Anka, Arte Johnson, Dick Cavett, Gloria Swanson, Jane Powell and Mickey Rooney, just to name a few at random. By the way, did you know that when movie studios need doubles for women to do stunts they often use small men?

Short stature doesn't limit or shut out many fields of endeavor. Communities are lowering the restrictions for policemen and firemen, and companies like General Motors have announced new programs (called "ergonomics") to adjust the comfort of working conditions to suit the size of the workers. Even small stewardesses can find jobs in small planes. Of course jockeys must be small, and we probably make better flagpole sitters too.

As discussed in Chapter 7, the hard part about finding a job is the social pressure against short stature. A motivated short person will put his employer and employees at ease by talking about it and clearing the air of any hidden curiosity and discomfort. Then the motivated person lets short stature help him in his work. A good example is how one disc jockey contended with the "Short People" record. As she told the *Wall Street Journal,* Sue O'Neill of WGCL in Cleveland, who is "almost" five feet tall, ran a counter-campaign around the song. She played it, but recorded her retorts and comments to the lyrics and played them voiced over Randy Newman's version. All the short people in Cleveland supported her cause, boosted her ratings, and wore, "I get small with Sue O'Neill" buttons.

It's interesting to note the paradox that although success is produced by talent, desire and competence—not size—short people are often motivated by their size to prove their talent, desire and competence! David Hornstein understood that when he wrote: "My life has been meaningful in greater measure than I ever dared to dream. I enjoy the happiest imaginable relationships with a host of friends and business associates. I think I have the respect of the community. I truly believe that all of these good things are just one big ball of wax, representing the natural consequence of the direction which my short stature gave to my life."

Do the advantages of being short outweigh the disadvantages? David Hornstein would say yes, because he used the advantages to their maximum and made light of the disadvantages. In other words, you control the scale, and it's up to you which side wins.

Short stature can be a positive force in helping you make something of yourself or it can be a great excuse for giving up. There are many excellent books on the market based on the "power of positive thinking" theme, which can be applied to every corner of our lives, from coping with short stature to, well, skiing.

The other day I read a review of *Inner Skiing* by Timothy Gallwey and Bob Kriegel. It's about the theory that everyone can ski better—or do anything better—if they can find a way to keep their fears, doubts and embarrassments from taking over their lives.

In his best-selling books about mind control, *Your Erroneous Zones* and *Pull Your Own Strings,* Dr. Wayne Dyer emphasizes that accepting your body is the first step in controlling your life. He reminds us, "You don't *have* a nice body; you *are* your body; and disliking it means not accepting yourself as a human being."

Accepting your short height is the first step in freeing you from a source of self-destructive behavior. Liking your short height, and letting it work for you instead of against you can promote great achievement and happiness. At the very least it can be minimized as a source of interference in reaching your life's goals.

Dr. Dyer contends that all feelings are based on thoughts, and since we can control our thoughts, we can control our feelings, especially those destructive feelings that threaten to ruin our lives. One of the great things about mind control is that you can work on it at any age. Did you spend an overprotected youth never coming to grips with your short height? Did your parents and teachers manage to knock down your self-image every time you bolstered it up? Has your shortness made you shy? Belligerent? Angry? Childish? Afraid? It's never too late to try to control the thoughts that control the feelings that control our lives. It's never too late to tip the scale so the advantages of being short outweigh the disadvantages.

First, make a list of the physical advantages and disadvantages as I did in this chapter, only use items that just apply to you in your personal, everyday life. Then decide how to "accentuate the positive and eliminate the negative." Second, tackle the psychological load. Are you letting being short work against you? How can you use your short height to full advantage—in your job, your social life, your hobbies, your community service, your family?

In the previous chapter I mentioned that it's a good idea for parents to supply their short children with ready answers to teasing and rude questions. Now I have a ready answer for any short person to the question, "Does your short height bother you?" I asked Cathy, my 5-foot, 18-year-old daughter that question not long ago, and her immediate reply was: "The advantages outweigh the disadvantages if you overlook the disadvantages." Isn't that beautiful?

You don't have to accept society's "bigger is better" judgment. Actually, the best time in our history to be short is right now. Think of all the effort going into solving growth problems and helping those with severe short stature. People all over the country researching, treating, testing, counseling, raising money for more research, collecting pituitary glands, lobbying for laws to help the disadvantaged. There are meetings, seminars, workshops, symposiums, conventions—all to do with some aspect of short stature.

Interest in growth is running high and short people are sure to benefit. Who knows, maybe someday "short is super" will be the byword. After all, we do require less space on this crowded planet, less food, less water, less energy to heat or cool or transport our smaller bodies, less fabric to clothe us. Maybe someday the engineers will lower all the chairs and counters and Douglas Taylor will run for President.

I'm not saying that short is better than tall or even better than average—how would I know that? I only know what it's like to be short, and I know it's important to grow as tall as heredity and environment and modern medicine will allow. But if you're short, discover how to use it to your advantage.

Then forget it.

Yes, that's what I said: F O R G E T   I T. I didn't say *deny* your shortness, I said forget it. A watched pot never boils. If you're consciously aware of your short stature it's bound to drag you down and bother you. If you notice it, good or bad, everyone else will too. If too much attention goes to your height, your mind and heart and soul might not grow, and they're far more interesting and worthy of attention than your height.

Don't you feel most alive when you've lost awareness of

yourself? It's a paradox, I know, but an ancient truth . . . by forgetting ourselves we find ourselves.

Short height is never a detriment to those who are so comfortable with their height that they forget they are short. I'm always shocked when I see myself in a photo with average-size people, or glimpse myself in a mirror standing next to someone. "Am I *that* short?" I ask myself. "Yes," I answer. And I forget about it again.

For months my short height's been held on a pin squirming under a magnifying glass while I've been working on this book. I've never spent so much time thinking about my shortness, and consequently I've never felt so small. I know I'll be more comfortable when I can forget about my height again, so let's end all this small talk. I could go on and on, but it's been my experience that it's best to keep things short, don't you agree?

Appendix

ORGANIZATIONS
CONCERNED WITH HUMAN GROWTH

HUMAN GROWTH FOUNDATION, INC.
Maryland Academy of Science Building
601 Light Street
Baltimore, Maryland 21230

LITTLE PEOPLE OF AMERICA, INC.
Box 126
Owatonna, Minnesota 55060

NATIONAL PITUITARY AGENCY
210 West Fayette Street
Baltimore, Maryland 21201

Index

Achondroplasia
  diagnosis of, 147
  employment and, 155–57
  and growth rate and motor development, 147–48
  inheritance pattern of, 136–39
  life expectancy and, 148
  LPA and, 149–54, 158
  mental ability and, 148
  parental acceptance of, 151–54
  and personality traits, 157–58
  physical symptoms of, 73, 135, 144–47
  problems with physical environment and, 143–44, 159
  reproduction and, 155
  self-acceptance of, 151–54, 157
  social acceptance of, 157–59
  social ostracism and, 148
  See also Little People of America; Dwarfism
Acromegaly, 84
Adolescence
  communication with parents in, 176–77
  delayed, 68–70, 178, 180–82
  growth spurt of, 13, 22, 38–39, 55–58, 60
  parental emotional support during, 178–82

Adolescence *(continued)*
  psychosocial problems of late, 13, 15, 69–70, 162, 178, 180–82
  and self-image, 177–82
  See also Puberty
Adrenal Glands
  hormonal stimulants of, 33, 35, 38
  location of, 33
  secretions of, 35, 38, 42
Adrenalin, 38
Adrenocorticotrophic hormone (ACTH), 35, 81
Advantages of short stature
  in business, 198–99
  physical, 191–92
  psychological, 195–99
  in sports, 192–94
Amino acids. *See* Protein
Amish, 128–29
Amniocentesis, 65, 140
Anatomical Gift Act, 87
Androgens, 38–39, 42, 70, 178. *See also* Adrenal Glands; Testes
Anka, Paul, 198
Anthropometry, 190
Apgar, Virginia, 121, 131
Arginine-Insulin Tolerance Test, 64
The Armor Within Us (Samachson), 44, 109

205

Autopsies
  declining rate in U.S., 87–88, 90
  in Europe, 94
  need for, 85, 90
The Awesome Worlds Within a Cell (National Geographic), 24

Balaban, Alvin, 84–86, 161, 165–66
Barty, Billy, 149, 153, 155
Beck, Joan, 121, 131
Bedou, Charles, 159
Bendix Corporation, 17–18
Berger, Melvin, 30
Birth Defects. *See* Congenital defects
Blizzard, Robert, 22, 55, 59, 68, 70, 76–77, 86, 92, 114–15, 124
Body Consciousness: You Are What You Feel (Fisher), 9
Body Size and Implications (Garn), 113–14
Bone
  age, 63–64
  disorders of, 44, 73, 135, 138, 144–48. *See also* Achondroplasia
  end of growth of, 36, 38–39, 42, 81–82
  hormones and, 35–39, 42, 44, 70
  nutrition and growth of, 106–09
  structure and growth of, 39–44
  X-rays and, 40, 63–64, 73, 147
Book of Lists, 83
Bowen, Georgia, 156
Breast feeding, 83, 110–11
Brothers, Joyce, 136
Bump, Lavinia (Mrs. Charles Stratton), 83, 127–28
Byrnes, Charles, 34

Cagney, James, 198
Calcitonin, 36–37, 39, 44
Calcium, 36–37, 43–44, 107–08
Caring For Your Unborn Child (Gots), 110
Carter, Jimmy, 18
Cavett, Dick, 198
Cells
  chromosomes in, 23–29, 119–20
  genes in, 23–29, 120
  growth and reproduction of, 21–22, 26–27, 120–23, 131
  hormonal regulation of, 31–39
  parts of, 29, 119–20
  protein synthesis in, 26–29
Chaplin, Charlie, 198
Children
  and developing self-image, 165–71, 179, 195
  and developing skills, 175, 193–94
  and help from parents, 78, 171–82
  and reactions to psychosocial problems, 162–66
  summary of major causes of short stature in, 67–77
  See also Adolescence; names of individual causes of short stature
Children of the Forest (TV show), 125
Choh, Hao Li, 34, 85
Chondrodystrophies, 73, 135, 138, 144, 147. *See also* Achondroplasia
Chromosomes
  in cellular reproduction, 119–23
  chemistry of, 23–29, 120
  congenital defects and, 75–76, 131–35
  in egg, 120–22
  number of, in cell, 23, 119–20
  sex, 120, 122–24, 134
  in sperm, 120–23
  See also DNA; Genes
Cloning, 140–41
Clothing, 168, 175, 188–89
Cole, Terry, 87–89, 118
Coming of Age In Samoa (Mead), 179
Communication
  between children and friends, 174–75, 195
  between doctors and patients, 61–62, 169–70
  between parents and children, 78, 151–53, 166–71, 176
  between parents and teachers, 173–74
  and teasing, nicknames, rudeness, 172–73, 195
  to ease prejudice, 197, 199

Congenital defects
  chromosomes and, 131–35
  drugs or illness and, 71, 130–31
  genes and, 127–31, 135–40
  March of Dimes and, 139
  parental age and, 132, 136–37
  short stature and, 127–40
  tests for, 140
Constitutional delayed growth, 68–70, 178, 180–81. *See also* Adolescence; Puberty
Conway, Tim, 6
Cooke, Robert, 141
Coolidge, Calvin, 18
Cortisone, 35, 38
Crawford, John, 95
Cretinism, 74, 111, 140
Crick, Francis, 23
Crosby, Bing, 192
Cushing, Harvey, 34

Daughaday, William, 74
Davis, Adelle, 109
Davis, Sammy, Jr., 198
Diet. *See* Nutrition
Disease. *See* Illness; names of individual illnesses
DNA (deoxyribonucleic acid)
  function of, as genetic code, 26–29, 106, 120
  research on recombinant, 140–42
  structure of, 23–25
  See also Genes
The Double Helix (Watson), 23
Down's syndrome, 131, 134, 140
Dreyfuss, Richard, 118
Driving, 154, 184, 188
Drugs, 71, 130
Dunn, Michael, 155–56
Dwarfism
  definition of, 18–19
  heredity and, 127–40, 155
  hypopituitary, 75, 79–83
  mental maturity and, 11, 148
  special problems of, 18, 143–59
  See also Achondroplasia
Dyer, Wayne, 200

Egg
  and birth defects, 131–32
  chromosomes in, 120, 123
  development of, 120–22
  See also Ovaries
Emotional problems, *See* Psychosocial short stature
Endocrine system, 31–39. *See also* Hormones; names of individual glands
Energy, 36, 91, 104
Environment
  genes and, 124–27
  growth and, 45, 103–17
  puberty and, 68
  See also Physical environment
Enzymes, 30–31
Enzymes In Action (Berger), 30
Erikson, Erik, 177
Estrogen, 38–39, 178. *See also* Ovaries
Exercise
  bone growth and, 43
  growth hormone and, 65, 91–92

Falkner, Frank, 5
Familial short stature. *See* Genetic short stature
Feeling Free (TV show), 174
Feldman, Saul, 8
Fels Research Institute, 50, 54–55, 66
Fetus. *See* Prenatal growth
Fisher, Seymour, 9
Food. *See* Nutrition

Gallwey, Timothy, 199–200
Garn, Stanley, 113–14
Genes
  chemistry of, 23–29, 120
  congenital defects and, 127–31, 135–40
  environment and, 124–27
  function of, 123–24
  Mendel's laws and, 123–24
  research on, 140–42
  transmission of, to offspring, 120–23
  See also Chromosomes; DNA

Genetic Code, 23–29, 120. *See also* DNA; Genes
Genetic counseling, 138–40
Genetic engineering, 140–42
Genetic short stature, 58–59, 94–95, 118–27. *See also* Heredity
Giantism, 83–84
Gonadotrophic hormones, 35, 38–39, 81–82, 89
Gonads
 hormonal secretions of, 35, 38–39, 178
 hormonal stimulants of, 33, 35, 38–39, 81–82
 hypothalamus and, 38–39
 location of, 33
 See also Testes; Ovaries
Good Housekeeping, 136
Gots, Barbara and Ronald, 110
Grey, Joel, 198
Growing Up (Tanner), 56–58
Growth (Life Science Library), 54, 58–59
Growth, catch-up
 after disease cure, 113–14
 after emotional deprivation, 116
 with growth hormone therapy, 81
 of small babies, 73
 with thyroid therapy, 74
Growth charts
 dangers of, 10
 at doctor's office, 48
 examples of average, 52–53
 how to use, 51–59
 as indicators of health, 10
 where to obtain, 51
 See also Growth rates
Growth hormone (HGH)
 adult pituitaries and, 90
 chemistry of, 85
 cost of, 89, 94
 deficiency of, 75, 79–83, 127–28
 See also Hypopituitarism
 distribution of, 86–87, 89
 emotions and, 115–17
 extraction of, from pituitary glands, 88–89
 function of, 34–35, 39, 84, 90–95
 genetic short stature and, 68, 94–95

Growth hormone *(continued)*
 94–95
 for growth therapy, 75, 79–81, 84–85, 89–91, 95, 98–102, 144
 imported, 94
 insulin and, 37, 91
 metabolism and, 35, 90–91, 93
 obesity and, 113
 overproduction of, 83–84
 prenatal growth and, 37, 80, 128
 pygmies and, 126
 research on, 85, 91–96
 sugar and, 91, 109–10
 supply of, for therapy and research, 86–90
 symposiums on, 75, 92, 95, 113
 synthesis of, 85
 tests to measure secretion of, 64–65
 uses of, besides growth therapy, 93–94
 See also National Pituitary Agency; Pituitary gland
Growth hormone releasing factor, 92
Growth problems
 danger signals of, 60–61
 summary of major, 67–77
 See also names of individual causes of short stature
Growth rates
 abnormal, 56, 58
 of adolescent spurt, 13, 22, 38–39, 55–58, 60
 average, 22, 52–61
 climate and, 126
 control of, 32. *See also* Hormones
 of different body parts, 36, 43, 55
 doctor's evaluation of, 62–66
 in genetic short stature, 68
 of girls vs. boys, 52–53, 55–57, 112–13
 growth charts and, 10, 51–53
 importance of checking, 46
 long-range trends in, 8, 58–59, 109, 113–15
 measurement of, 47–53
 seasonal variations in, 50–51
 standard deviations of, 56
 velocity of, 56

Growth rates *(continued)*
  See also names of individual causes of short stature
Growth studies
  on achondroplasia and paternal age, 136
  and anthropometry, 190
  on athletes, 192
  on average U.S. adult height, 4, 8, 54
  on bone disorders, 147
  on Down's syndrome and maternal age, 131–32
  on emotional support, 179
  on employment and height, 17
  at Fels Research Institute, 54–55
  on growth rates of girls vs. boys, 112–13
  on height prediction, 66
  on growth hormone and blood sugar, 91
  on growth-hormone chemistry, 73
  on growth hormone and non-hypopituitary dwarfs, 95
  on growth-hormone therapy for diseases other than growth problems, 93–94
  and Human Growth Foundation, 95–96
  on human milk and thyroid hormone, 111
  on inheritance patterns of recessive genes, 127–29
  and Little People of America, 150
  on long-range trends of growth rates, 58–59, 105
  on malnutrition in U.S., 105, 110–12
  on muscle-cell growth in boys vs. girls, 112
  on newborn with lack of insulin, 37
  on nutrition therapy, 104–05
  on obesity, 113–14
  on parental reaction, 171
  on perceived height, 16–17
  on personality problems of hypopituitary children, 165–66, 169
  on personality traits of dwarfs, 158

Growth studies *(continued)*
  on prematurity and protein synthesis, 111
  on prenatal growth and alcohol, 71
  on psychological problems of dwarfs, 18, 166
  on psychosocial short stature, 115–16
  on sequence of events of puberty, 57
  on somatomedin, 92–93
  on somatostatin and GH-releasing factor, 92
Grunt, Jerome, 98–99
Guillemin, Roger, 92
Guinness Book of World Records, 83
Gurdon, John, 141

Hall, Judith, 137, 146
Hayles, Alvin, 46
Height
  and age, 10–11, 63–64, 148, 161
  inherited potential of, 124
  measuring, 47–51
  and mental maturity, 10–11, 148
  predicting, 66
  as racial characteristic, 125–27
  and respect, 16–17
  and self-image, 9–10, 165, 177–79, 195–97
  See also Growth rates; names of individual causes of short stature
Heightism, 8, 15. *See also* Prejudice
Helping Parents Cope With Children of Short Stature (Spector), 170
Heredity
  congenital defects and, 127–40
  dwarfism and, 127–40, 155
  environment and, 124–27
  genes and, 120–24, 127–40
  puberty and, 68
  short stature and, 118–42
  See also Chromosomes; DNA; Genes
The Heredity Factor (Nyhan), 138–39
HEW (Dept. of Health, Education & Welfare)
  1976 study on average heights, 4, 8, 54
  report on child suicides, 163

HEW (continued)
  studies on malnutrition, 105, 110–11
Hickey, John, 7
Hoffman, Dustin, 118, 198
Hoffman, William, 48, 50, 64, 95
Hormones
  bone growth and, 35–39, 42, 44, 70
  function of, 31–39
  hypothalamus and, 35–36, 38, 92, 117, 128, 141
  research and, 91–96
  See also names of individual endocrine glands and hormones
Hormones: How They Work (Riedman), 36
Hornstein, David, 195–99
Howard, Ted, 141
How Children Grow (NIH), 38, 41, 55, 112, 147
How To Live Through Junior High School (Johnson), 176–77
Human Genetics (McKusick), 127–28, 136
Human Growth Foundation, Inc. (HGF), 7–8, 46, 60, 68, 73, 84, 86–88, 95–96, 134, 147, 149, 161, 170–71, 195
Hunter, John, 34
Hutterites, 128
Hypopituitarism, 75, 79–86, 89–91, 100–02, 127–28. See also Growth hormone
Hypothalamus, 35–36, 38, 92, 117, 128, 141
Hypothyroidism, 74, 111, 140

Identity. See Self-image
Illness, 77, 104–05, 110–11, 114. See also Congenital defects; names of individual illnesses
Improving on Nature (Cooke), 141
Improving Your Child's Behavior Chemistry (Smith), 170–71
Inherited short stature. See Genetic short stature
Inner Skiing (Gallwey and Kriegel), 199–200

Insulin, 37, 39, 80, 91
Intrauterine growth retardation, 71–73, 96–100, 166–69
Irving, Washington, 18
Is My Baby All Right? (Apgar and Beck), 121, 131

James At 16 (TV show), 118
Jewell, Catherine, 12, 15, 47, 180, 194, 201
Jewell, Linda, 15–16, 177, 180, 185
Johnson, Arte, 198
Johnson, Eric, 176–77

Kerlan, Robert, 192
Kitchens, Lee, 152–54, 157
Kitchens, Mary, 154
Kriegel, Bob, 199–200
Kwashiorkor, 104–05, 110–11

Landers, Ann, 173
Lawrence, Steve, 6
Leachman, Cloris, 157
Let's Eat Right To Keep Fit (Davis), 109
Life, 156
Little People of America, Inc. (LPA), 19, 149–54, 158–59, 197
Lobsenz, Norman, 179
Longfellow, Henry Wadsworth, 160
Lorre, Peter, 198

McKusick, Victor, 127–28, 136
Madison, James, 18
Marasmus, 104–05, 110–11
March of Dimes, 139
Mead, Margaret, 179
Meanwhile Back at the Womb—Growth Retardation (Perrin), 71, 73
Medical World News, 46, 61, 115, 180
Mendel, Gregor Johann, 123
Menstruation
  average age of start of, 56–57, 59
  growth spurt and, 56
  obesity and, 113
  See also Adolescence; Puberty
Michu, 75–76
Midgets. See Dwarfism
Molnar, Stephen, 126

Index

Money, John, 11, 157, 162–63, 172
Mongolism. *See* Down's syndrome
Morris, Barbara, 154–55, 174
Morris, Brian, 4–5, 143, 154–55, 157–59
Mosier, David, Jr., 92, 95
Murphy, Calvin, 194
Musters, Pauline, 83
Mutations, 130–32, 136–40. *See also* Congenital defects
Muth, Harriet, 180–82, 198
My Child Is A Dwarf (Rogers and Weiss), 151

Napoleon, 17
National Geographic Magazine, 24
National Institutes of Health (NIH), 38, 41, 55, 69, 95, 103–04, 111–14, 147
National Pituitary Agency (NPA), 86–92
Newman, Paul, 118
Newman, Randy, 6–7, 199
Niall, Hugh, 85
Nutrition
  bone growth and, 106–09
  in boys vs. girls, 112–13
  calories and, 103–04, 112
  deficiency in, 104–05, 110–11
  emotions and, 116
  long-range growth trends and, 58, 105
  malabsorption and, 114–15
  minerals and, 106, 108–09
  overfeeding and, 58, 112–14
  prenatal and infant, 110–11
  protein and, 104–06
  vitamins and, 106–09
Nutritional short stature, 75. *See also* Nutrition
Nyhan, William, 138–39

Obesity
  dwarfism and, 146
  growth hormone and, 113
  menstruation and, 113
  nutrition and, 113–14
Oliver, Grace, 153–54
O'Neill, Sue, 199

Ovaries
  egg development in, 120–23
  hormonal regulation of, 35, 38–39, 81–82
  secretions of, 35, 38–39, 178
  See also Egg; Estrogen; Gonads

Pacino, Al, 198
Pancreas, 33, 37
Panhypopituitarism, 81–82
Parathormone, 37, 39, 44
Parathyroid Glands, 37, 44
Parent, Dan, 81
Parents
  and children's self-image, 166–71
  helping achondroplastic children, 151–53
  helping short children cope, 78, 171–82
Patek, Fred, 194
Pathologists
  letters to, thanking for pituitary glands, 100–02
  role of, in obtaining pituitary glands, 84, 86–89
Patterns of Growth (HGF), 68
People, 7, 152
Perrin, Eugene, 65, 71, 73
Phosphorus, 24, 43–44, 107–08
Phyllis (TV show), 157
Physical environment
  problems of, in home, 12, 171, 190; in public places, 12–13, 143–44, 159, 171–72, 183–84, 190; in school, 11–12, 172
Pituitary gland
  control of adrenal glands, 33, 35, 38
  control of gonads, 33, 35, 38, 81–82
  control of thyroid gland, 33, 35–36
  and growth hormone, 34–35. *See also* Growth hormone
  how to donate, 87–88
  hypothalamus and, 35–36, 38, 92, 117, 128, 141
  location of, 33
  pathologists and, 84, 86–89, 100–02

Pituitary gland *(continued)*
  problems of obtaining, 84–90
  See also names of individual hormones
PKU (phenylketonuria), 31
Player, Gary, 118
Powell, Jane, 198
Prejudice
  achondroplastic dwarfs and, 143–44, 148
  coping with, 20, 171–82, 195–202
  in employment and business, 17–18, 198
  language and, 8
  in politics, 18
  public awareness of, 7
  in relating size to age, 10–11, 148, 161
  in schools, 11–15, 173–74
  and self-image, 10, 165
  Short People record and, 6–7
  short people's susceptibility to, 7
  in trite remarks, nicknames, questions, 13, 172–73, 195
  See also Psychosocial problems
Prenatal growth
  causes of abnormal, 71, 110
  controlling factors of, 37, 80, 128
  prematurity and, 71
  retardation of, 71–73
  testing procedures of, 65, 140
Progesterone, 38. *See also* Ovaries
Protein
  body growth and, 29–31, 104–06
  cell manufacture of, 26–29
  as component of bone, 41
  deficiency of, effect of on growth, 75, 104–06
  See also Enzymes; Hormones; Nutrition
Psychosocial problems
  help from parents for, 151–53, 171–82
  how to cope with, 195–202
  overconcern about height and, 61, 201
  reactions to, of short children, 162–66
  and self-image, 165–71, 195

Psychosocial problems *(continued)*
  of slow sexual maturation, 13, 15, 69–70, 162, 178, 180–82
  See also Prejudice
Psychosocial short stature, 77, 115–17
Puberty
  beginning of, 38–39, 56–57, 61
  decrease in pubertal age, 58–59
  delayed, 68–70, 178, 180–82
  female growth and, 55–57
  heredity vs. environment and, 68
  male growth and, 55–57
  menstruation and, 56–57, 59, 113
  physical changes of, 39, 55–57
  See also Adolescence
Pull Your Own Strings (Dyer), 200
Pygmies, 125–27

Raben, Maurice, 84–85, 88
Races, 125–27
Races, Types and Ethnic Groups (Molnar), 126
Radioimmunoassay, 32, 82
Raiti, Salvatore, 35, 89–90, 94, 116
Rasa, Gerald, 7
Redford, Robert, 118
Rehabilitation Literature (Money), 162–63, 172
Reproductive cells. *See* Egg; Sperm
Riedman, Sarah, 36
Rifkin, Jeremy, 141
Ringling Bros.-Barnum & Bailey Circus, 75–76, 82–83, 118
Rimoin, David, 127–28
RNA (ribonucleic acid), 28–29
Robinson, Edward G., 198
Roche, Alex, 66
Rooney, Mickey, 142, 198

Samachson, Joseph, 44, 109
Sauls, Henry, 68, 97–98, 167, 171
Schools
  help for short children in, 172–74
  problems for short children in, 11–15
Scientific American (Tanner), 56–58
Scott, Charles, 19, 136, 138, 146–47, 149–50, 155, 174

Secular trend. *See* Growth rates, long-range trends in
Self-image
  and adolescence, 177–82
  body size and, 9–10, 165, 177–79, 195–97
  and clothing, 168, 175
  hypopituitary children and, 165–66, 169
  parents and, 166–71, 180–82
  and self-acceptance, 151–54, 157, 200
  and skills, 175
  See also Psychosocial problems
Sex hormones. *See* Androgens; Estrogen
Sexual Maturation. *See* Adolescence; Puberty
Shoemaker, Bill, 192
Shortest human, 83
Short People (song), 6–7, 199
Simon, Paul, 198
Sleep, 91, 116–17
Smith, Lendon, 170–71
Social Development of Dwarfs (Weiss), 18, 166
Somatomedin (SM), 92–93
Somatostatin, 92, 141–42
Somatotrophin. *See* Growth hormone
Spector, Steven, 170
Sperm
  and birth defects, 132, 136–37
  chromosomes in, 120
  development of, 120–23
  See also Testes
Sports, 168, 192–94
Statistics
  on achondroplasia, 18, 144, 146
  on average adult heights, male and female, 4, 8
  on average growth rate, 22, 52–53, 55
  on children with growth problems, 5
  on Down's syndrome and maternal age, 131
  on HGF funds for growth research, 95–96

Statistics *(continued)*
  on hypopituitary children, 84, 89
  on long-range trends in growth rates, 58–59
  on malnutrition, 104–05
  on pituitary-gland collection, 89
  on pubertal age, 55–56
  on short females, 4
  on Turner's syndrome, 132
Stevens, Howard, 194
Stratton, Charles (General Tom Thumb), 82–83, 127–28
Strudwick, John, 148–49, 151–52, 157
Sugar
  growth hormone and, 91, 109–10
  insulin and, 37
Swanson, Gloria, 198

Tallest living man, 83
Tallest living woman, 83–84
Tallest man, 59, 83
Tanner, James, 48, 50, 56–58
Taylor, Barbara, 96–100, 166–70
Taylor, Douglas, 46, 71, 96–100, 166–69, 173, 194, 201
Teenagers. *See* Adolescence; Puberty
Testes
  hormonal regulation of, 35, 38–39, 81–82
  secretions of, 35, 38–39, 178
  sperm development in, 120–23
  See also Androgens; Gonads; Sperm
Testosterone, 38–39, 42, 70, 178. *See also* Adrenal glands; Testes
Thissen, David, 66
Thompson, Robert, 98
Thyroid gland
  hormones and, 35–37, 44
  hormone deficiency of, 74, 111, 140
  location of, 33
Thyrotrophin (TSH), 35, 74, 81, 89
Thyroxine, 36. *See also* Thyroid gland
Time, 194
Tom Thumb (Charles Stratton), 82–83, 127–28
Turner's syndrome, 76–77, 132–35

Underwood, Louis, 46, 48
Uniform Donor Card, 87–88

VanderLaan, Willard, 113
VanWyk, Judson, 93, 180
Villechaize, Herve, 156
Vitamin D-resistant rickets, 108, 139

Wadlow, Robert, 59, 83
Wainer, Howard, 66
Walker, Nancy, 198
Wall Street Journal, 7, 199
Watson, James D., 23
Watusis, 125–27

Weldon, Virginia, 61, 179
Weiss, Joan, 18, 151, 166, 170
Whitney, Honor, 179
Who Should Play God? (Howard and Rifkin), 141
Williams, Paul, 198
Woman's Day, 179

X-rays
  bone growth and, 40, 63–64, 73, 147
  mutations and, 130

Your Erroneous Zones (Dyer), 200